BRAIN
POWER

C. SAMUEL VERGHESE, M.D., PH.D.
Forewords by Clancy D. McKenzie, M.D. and
John A. Hash, Litt.D., D.D.

BRAIN POWER

How to

Fine-Tune

Your Brain

Naturally

WINEPRESS **WP** PUBLISHING

WinePress Publishing (PO Box 428, Enumclaw, WA 98022) functions only as book publisher. As such, the ultimate design, content, editorial accuracy, and views expressed or implied in this work are those of the author.

All Scripture quotations, unless otherwise indicated, are taken from the Holy Bible, translated by the author. The purpose of the translation was to render a contemporary, easy-to-read English text regarding the mind and related subjects. The author used the Masoretic Text of the Hebrew Bible as represented in Biblica Hebraica Stuttgartensia (1977); The Greek New Testament, published by the USB fourth revised edition, 1993; Vine's complete Expository Dictionary of the Old and New Testament Words, and New Strong's Exhaustive Concordance of the Bible Including Greek and Hebrew Dictionaries. All are published by Thomas Nelson Publishers, Nashville, Tennessee.

DISCLAIMER: Every effort has been made to ensure that the information contained in this book is accurate and current. The ideas, procedures and suggestions are not intended as a substitute for consulting with your physician. Matters pertaining to health often require medical supervision. Neither the author, Natures Hospital staff, nor the Integrative Medicine and Biofeedback Clinic, shall be liable for any damage, injury or loss allegedly arising from any of the suggestions or products recommended in this book, telephone conversations, E-mails, web sites, or radio and TV discussions suggestions, preparations or anything else.

Brain images by Samuel Verghese and Tom Rosa: Tommyproductions.com; 1.800.694.7770

ISBN 13: 978-1-57921-889-8
ISBN 10: 1-57921-889-X
Library of Congress Catalog Card Number: 2006940451

1. Nutritional healing 2. Spiritual healing 3. Psychology 4. Brain 5. Mind 6. Christ-likeness

Printed in Colombia.

Contents

Endorsements for
How to Fine-Tune Your
Brain Naturally

I heartily recommend *How to Fine-Tune Your Brain Naturally.* It speaks holistically and convincingly to your life—body, mind, and spirit—with healing guidance by a true authority. I believe you and your brain are what you eat; have you heard that food goes straight to your head? The practical information in this book elevates this truth to a powerful therapeutic tool. The ninth chapter provides sample meal plans for an entire week; this alone is worth the price of the entire volume—and there is so much more!"

—Ben Armstrong, Ph.D., M. Div.,
Former Ex. Dir., Nat. Religious Broadcasters;
Hall of Fame Winner for NRB, 1998;
Dir. of Doctoral Prog.,
Faith Theological Seminary, Baltimore, MD

"Allow me to address the man before the book. I have known Dr. Verghese for many years. We have ministered together at home and on the foreign field. He has been my doctor, driving disease from my body and keeping me healthy. At times he has also been my spiritual doctor. Dr. Verghese is a devout Christian who practices what he preaches. St. Paul tells us to let the mind that was in Christ also be in us. To have a proper attitude, a healthy mind is essential—*How to Fine-Tune Your Brain Naturally* will significantly aid you in achieving that. I recommend this book to you wholeheartedly."

—J. Bruce Sofia, M.Ed., D.D.,
Founder and Senior Pastor,
Gloucester County Community Church,
Washington Twp., NJ;
teacher on *Changed by the Word* radio program;
host of *The Other Side* TV broadcast;
author of numerous *Ask the Pastor* pamphlets.

"This latest book by Dr. Verghese is a ground-breaking volume by an extraordinary healer. As a clinician, I have seen first-hand the work that he has done with patients, such as a gentlemen with an appalling infestation of winged parasites throughout his body. This man had been to some of our nation's finest medical centers for evaluation and treatment; none were able to successfully treat him. In Dr. Verghese's care, his condition improved significantly after initial treatment with herbal formulations in just two weeks. Dr. Verghese's integration of the spiritual into the healing process is profound. This book is essential reading for all in the helping professions and for laypersons wishing to better themselves."

—Bruce A. Naylor, Ph.D.,
Licensed Psychologist,
former asst. prof. of counseling,
Eastern University

"I suffered severe symptoms of hyperthyroidism—including rapid heartbeat, nervousness, irritability, fatigue, hand tremors and weight loss. My family physician confirmed my diagnosis and referred me to an endocrinologist, who prescribed medications that made me very sick. My blood test results again showed high levels of the hormone. I was wary of treatment with radioactive iodine, and I didn't wish to rush into surgery to remove my thyroid gland. My husband Steven and I turned to Dr. Verghese for alternative treatment. Within a short period of time, my disease improved dramatically, and I have remained asymptomatic for the past several years."

—LuAnn Morrow, D.C., CCRD
and Steven G. Schram, D.C., CA., DAAPM, NMS
Chiropractic and Acupuncture Clinic

Disclaimer

E very effort has been made to ensure that the information contained in this book is accurate and current. The ideas, procedures and suggestions are not intended as a substitute for consulting with your physician. Matters pertaining to health often require medical supervision. Neither the author, Nature's Hospital staff, nor the Integrative Medicine and Biofeedback Clinic shall be liable for any damage, injury, or loss allegedly arising from any of the suggestions or products recommended in this book, telephone conversations, e-mails, Web sites, or radio and TV discussions, suggestions, preparations or anything else.

Integrative Medicine & Biofeedback Clinic
813 East Gate Dr, Suite B
Mt. Laurel, NJ 08054
1-888-661-2827
www.biofeedbacknj.com

Foreword

Volume One of *How to Fine-Tune Your Brain Naturally* is an extraordinary exposition on how to do precisely that. Its success is based on three essential components: Holy Scriptures, medical knowledge, and compassion.

Holy Scriptures provide the foundation for all healing: with pure love, forgiveness, and freedom from conflict, people avoid the damaging effects of stress, bitterness, anger, hatred, and depression. Love heals all and prevents illness and imbalances in our bodies, minds, and souls.

The second critical factor is a comprehensive knowledge of integrative medicine. This is the frontier of modern medicine, and Dr. Verghese leads the way. Instead of treating symptoms, he identifies and treats causes, while cautioning against the harmful effects of medication.

The third and most important ingredient is compassion. Dr. Verghese comes from a long line of dedicated Christian servants who accomplished their work without government funding, but continue to serve people in various capacities. This is a family of givers, with love and compassion for all. Thus, when Dr. Verghese develops a new formula for fine-tuning any part of the body, I am confident it is prepared strictly for the purpose of healing. In contrast, industry too often serves two masters, the most compelling of which is their "bottom line."

For example, joint preparations found on the shelves of health food stores have prominent labels using current "buzzwords" that sell, such as "chondroitin" or "glucosamine." Dr. Verghese's joint preparation simply is called "natural joint integrity," but it contains 25 ingredients. If he were to recommend 25 different herbs and nutrients for joint disease, no one would follow it. Thus, he must recommend his own products.

Dr. Verghese's specialty is brain function, which is one more reason why Volume One of *Brain Power: Fine-Tuning Your Brain Naturally* is a very special contribution to mankind's quest for health and establishing a relationship with our Creator.

—*Dr. Clancy D. McKenzie, M.D.*
Professor of Integrative Medicine

Foreword

As Founder and President of Bible Pathway Ministries, I am happy to commend this timely book to you. Information in the Christian world on this vital subject is sadly lacking.

Using as examples some of the patients he has helped, Dr. Verghese describes their symptoms and the treatment rendered to provide relief so they could pursue Christ-likeness. He is well qualified to write on the subject of the brain; it has been a lifelong passion. He has received training from various academic institutions.

The ultimate goal is to bring those who are hurting into a healthy physical and spiritual state. As our minds are brought to a full healthy functioning, we are able to grow in spiritual depth and fruitful service to the Lord. Failure to recognize and correct symptoms of mental imbalance can limit our spiritual effectiveness and service to the Lord. Dr. Falwell states, "Becoming more like Christ is Dr. Sam Verghese's prayer and passion."

As part of this instructive book, a whole chapter, "Foods to Fine-tune Your Brain," is devoted to wholesome diet. You will find this book a very practical one for personal application.

I unreservedly recommend this book to those who desire to be fruitful in the Kingdom of God.

—Dr. John Hash, Litt.D., D.D.
President, Bible Pathway Ministries

Preface

I n recent years there has been a groundswell of interest in alternatives to orthodox medicine. This movement away from godless, toxic, mechanistic medicine is not only salutary—it is essential to man's spiritual progress. Through the centuries, the interventions of conventional medicine have done much to sicken humanity and weaken the human gene pool. It seems that, with few exceptions, the more effective these interventions, the more disastrous their consequences. This is simply because medical orthodoxy lacks an understanding of health and disease and offers no theory or *modus operandi* of cure. Essentially, medical orthodoxy is a powerful, entrenched body of ignorance to be overcome. God's Word on this subject is blunt and clear: "Do you realize that you are a temple of God and that God's Spirit lives in you? God will destroy anyone who destroys this temple of God. For God's temple is holy, and you are that temple" (1 Corinthians 3:16–17).

True to the human condition, the deluge of herbal and nutritional supplements, combination of homeopathic remedies, essential oils, and the like (many with exaggerated claims) confront the consumer with a bewildering plethora of possibilities. Many have spent thousands of dollars on supplements without achieving the relief and renewal they sought. Many have spent years of research without gaining the crucial judgment necessary to know what works and how to apply it.

There is no conceit to assert that about 50 years ago God began preparing one of His humble servants for the complex task of providing natural healing and the information necessary to use the bounties of the earth wisely for self-healing. In my estimation, Dr. Verghese has done a superb job of providing a reliable compass to earnest seekers and suffering humanity. I admire his wealth of knowledge, and as his friend and professional colleague, I have learned a great deal. I know that I have only scratched the surface of his reservoir of knowledge and wisdom of herbs, nutrients, and neurophysiology. It is endearing that Sam often begins the answer to one of my questions with, "As you know," when in fact, I didn't know or had forgotten. Always supportive, empowering, and kind-hearted, he has been a blessing in my life.

Dr. Verghese may speak in similar terms of my editorial acumen. I feel privileged that I am able to contribute to the dissemination of this high-quality guidance.

Future volumes are in various stages of preparation. I envision these books undergoing revision and being re-issued as dictated by growing knowledge, feedback, and demand from readers. I also envision an international army of physicians well trained in the strategies vouchsafed in this book and future volumes, available to help those whose difficulties are beyond self-help.

Finally, this effort has its priorities right. Radiant health is only an interim goal, providing the most solid foundation for the quintessential goal of spiritual growth—manifesting the life of Jesus Christ in our daily walk.

—Dr. James F. Claire, D.O.

Acknowledgements

I t is difficult to even begin to adequately acknowledge those
who invested in my life. Most importantly, I express my
indebtedness and gratitude to the triune God for allowing me
to write this book. I humbly dedicate this work first to the
Lord Jesus Christ, my Creator, Savior, and Lord. I am indebted
to my family: my dear wife, Rita, for her unstinting, selfless
efforts in typing the manuscript over and over as it evolved;
second, to my children, Sam, Ben, and Rachael; third, to my
godly grandparents and to my parents, Pastor and Mrs. C.V.
Samuel; and fourth, my sisters Jessica and Alice; and my brothers, Abraham, Isaac, and their families.

A special thanks is due to my good friend and clinical part-
ner, James F. Claire, D.O., who edited and enriched the text
with many insights. Likewise, thanks to my dear pastor and
friend, Dr. J. Bruce Sofia, founder and senior pastor of Gloucester County Community Church, Sewell, New Jersey; K.O.
George, M.D., President of Hahnemann School of Homeopathic Medicine, for enlarging my understanding during my

years as a medical student and instructor. I am further grateful to Jim and Florence Biros, and Dr. John and Ann Norris for their friendship, prayers, and encouragement in bringing this book to fruition. Lastly, my thanks to three groups of people: members of Christ's Body at large; patients whose sufferings and victories I have witnessed, and numerous Christ-like believers, who have encouraged me in this endeavor.

Introduction

I t all happened about 50 years ago. I remember the vivid images and moving visual perceptions of Christ's life and death on the cross for us. The invasion of the Holy Spirit into my life installed in an abiding place a compulsive desire for God and a love for people. At the age of five, living and working with my parents, who were Christian missionaries in Southern India, I began to acquire the knowledge and experience that would one day bear fruit in many nutritional formulations and the information in this book. At home, a steady stream of people came through our doors—some with mental illnesses. Christians, Hindus, Muslims and others; some lived in our home to receive help. The variety of help provided for these people was as diverse as their challenges. Some were clearly under the control of Satan and needed primarily spiritual healing. Others needed supportive spiritual guidance accompanied by nutritional, naturopathic, ayurvedic, homeopathic and/or traditional medicines.

It was heart-wrenching to see the mental suffering of these people. Even at my young age, I yearned to contribute to their healing. Some recovered fully and continued their spiritual journey. Many recovered partially and did their best to live fully. Still others made little progress. Their brains were so disordered that their lives were indescribably miserable. These things I witnessed and contemplated as I was growing up.

During my teen years, through the influence of the Bible and my involvement in assisting many people who recovered by God's grace, I became convinced that it was possible to change the brain's functional and structural abnormalities through the above mentioned means to improve the health of the mind and facilitate spiritual growth toward Christ-likeness.

During my years of higher academic learning, especially in the 1970s, I was often intensely frustrated by the inadequacy and fallacies of the prevalent mechanistic and evolutionary models of the brain that were taught by scientists and intellectuals of our educational institutions.[1] At that time discoveries in neuroscience were few; conventional practitioners were not able to effectively help most people with mental dysfunction.[2] In addition, as it has been in the past, many Christians also used the crude methods of the world in their teaching and treatment of the mentally disabled. Eventually, with God's grace, I embarked on research of natural treatment modalities for people with brain deficits, based on the time-tested, biblical model of healing, clinical experience, and a reliable body of sound experimental evidence from eminent scientists throughout the world. At the time, healing information through natural remedies in the United States was difficult to acquire.

---

[1] In the evolutionary model of the brain, it evolved from the bottom up: first, the base of the brain, referred to as the reptilian brain; second, the paleomammalian brain; third, the neomammalian brain or cortex.

[2] Vol. II will explore examples of the biblical model of mental healing.

Thirty-five years ago, as I was learning neuroscience, I discovered that the biblical information about man's brain and mind was far ahead of the neurosciences and that the creation of the complex brain stood as one of the major evidences that God is a Creator with infinite intelligence and power. And yet neuroscientists were wasting time, talent, and resources by developing fanciful hypotheses about how the amazingly complex human brain might have evolved.

My desire to find ways to induce joy into the lives of suffering souls continued. The neurobiochemical changes in the brains of mentally suffering Christians undergoing natural treatment fascinated me, and the consequent transformation of people newly able to emulate Christ with Holy Spirit-inspired joy was rewarding and inspiring. The spiritual healing of demon-controlled individuals and their subsequent improved mental health was equally thrilling. How does this happen? What spiritual and neurobiochemical process took place in their brains? I am still interested in research and in discovering new ways to help people.

After our marriage, my wife and I continued in my parents' footsteps in the USA, opening our home to a few troubled souls, including former cult members whose lives had been wrecked by illegal drugs or satanic forces. Many of these youngsters had become bored with lifeless traditional churches and had embraced Eastern mysticism against the will of their parents. Discipling such people was part of my life in India; it was always extremely challenging because they vigorously rejected traditional Christianity. Reaching these people was intense and exhausting; the journey was stormy, and occasionally our lives were threatened by various cult members. But it was amazing how, once their brains were balanced, most of these people were able to think clearly; these newcomers to the family of God leaped for joy in following Christ's path.

It is not surprising that the writing of this book, begun in the sixties in India, is still a work in progress because of the recent rapid growth of understanding of the complex functions of the brain, the arduous work of determining the gene-modifying action of thousands of herbs and nutrients on brain functioning, and the need to integrate neurobiological, psychological, spiritual, and behavioral perspectives to create an effective means of helping those in need.

Neuroscience has been slowly discovering that genetic heredity and early life environmental influences do not consign human beings to a limited or predictable fate. Genes and in particular genetic functioning are far more plastic and adaptable than scientists believed a short time ago. Genes are the structural reservoirs of the information needed for the development and maintenance of the physical organism and many of its nonphysical characteristics. However, without the quickening, intelligent power of the life energy—God's breath—the organism would be only an inert, readily perishable conglomeration of organic chemicals. If genes and character were immutable, there would be no spiritual new birth, no growth into Christ-likeness, no hope, no miracles, and no possibility of notably advancing the science of brain healing. The Bible clearly teaches that through the transforming power of Jesus Christ and by means of God-given remedial substances, the possibility of transforming ourselves through the work of the Holy Spirit is real. The Scriptures also make it clear that it is our responsibility to seek such a transformation with the specific aim of becoming like Christ. We are to clearly manifest the will of God in all our thoughts and deeds. This book is my humble contribution to that exalted calling.

Natural biochemical modulation of the brain and correction of malfunctioning genes are relatively new tools that have been brought to this work. The combinations of herbs and all scientific treatment possibilities to promote healthy functioning of the body, with particular attention to the brain and nervous system, are new and now readily accessible to the sincere pilgrim. They can help to clear obstructions to the spiritual life by supporting and nourishing the body's capacity to heal itself. God created our bodies with wonderful resilience and transformative powers. Once these gross physical and psychological obstructions are removed, the lion's share of the aspirant's work lies ahead. One must use the tools of will, mind, conscience, prayer, meditation, group worship, contemplation, right thought, and action, spurred on by God's grace, the work of the Holy Spirit, and the boundless love of the Lord Jesus Christ. And that is why this book is a humble contribution. Beyond that, you will apply your God-given resurrection power to stand on the Solid Rock that is Christ and be transformed into Christ-likeness.

Let there be no misunderstanding: there is no herb, no vitamin, no pill, or pharmaceutical agent that can substitute for the work of the Holy Spirit. In these pages you will find practical, natural strategies to up-regulate or down-regulate cellular functioning or molecular actions to facilitate balanced operation of the body, that in turn facilitate the attainment of joyful Christian living. The activation and deactivation of the cells, in turn, either activate or deactivate our brain and the rest of the body systems. The imitation of Christ is an ascending, never-ending task; no matter how Christ-like you are at a particular moment, there is always a higher level to reach until you see Him face to face in all His glory.

The many nutritional prescriptions and other recommendations presented in this book have worked for thousands of people in achieving true "brain power." "That is, to become more like the Lord Jesus. I have seen many personal breakthroughs, many earnest people emerging from suffering to rejoice in the radiant brilliance of God's love. These practical ideas can be applied to personal, family, and business lives. The Christian life is an exciting journey because ultimately you are committing your whole being to following the footsteps of the Lord Jesus Christ, "the supreme example of humility and selfless concern for others" (Philippians 2:5-8).

It is my earnest prayer that God will continue to richly bless you with radiant health, infuse you with inner strength (Philippians 4:13), and suffuse your life with Christ's love (Ephesians 3:19).

> Let all people who look to God be joyful and happy because of what He has accomplished.
>
> —Psalm 70:4

> Fruit trees of all kinds will grow along the banks of the river . . . water will flow from the throne of God to the trees . . . and they will always bear fruit.
> They will be for food and their leaves for medicine.
>
> —Ezekiel 47:12

Chapter One

Healing from Brain, Hormonal, and Inherited Imbalances

By the grace of our Lord Jesus Christ, Joyce J. reversed her brain fog, sadness, grief, hormone imbalance, anxiety, depression, and lack of passion for God into rejoicing in the Holy Spirit. She was able to break through the disabling imbalance that loomed like an ominous cloud to experience her God-given life energy flowing abundantly and harmoniously.

She had sought Christian pastoral and psychological counseling before her symptoms became severe. At the time of her visit to our clinic, she was still seeing a psychiatrist and a Christian counselor. Here's a condensed version of her story.

NO MORE READY SMILE

On a Thursday afternoon about 3:00 P.M., Joyce came with her husband to see me. This was her first visit. Her husband, Jack, vice-president of a defense contracting firm, had his right arm wrapped around Joyce's shoulders. He introduced his wife and himself and sat down. She had with her a stack of papers containing her own notes and treatment reports.

Joyce, 51, looking weary and older than her age, gave me a friendly smile. I could sense misery behind her smile. Jack said, "Well, initially I called and talked with you because our minister recommended you, and a friend of ours had come to see you." After a pause, Jack said, "When I first met Joyce 25 years ago she was a robust, cheery, bright, take-charge kind of person. She was pursuing her business degree in graduate school. She always had a ready smile. She loved the Lord and you could see His work of grace in her life."

Then Joyce asked, "Doctor, please tell me how you can help me. I have seen many doctors over three years . . . something like that . . . and it has been quite a painful journey." (Pause) I explained to her what my specific treatment protocol for her would be and then added, "I will do my best through God's help to be of service to you until you recover and I will earnestly ask God to heal you."

A GLIMPSE OF VIBRANCY

Something changed in Joyce's eyes when she heard that and her face began to glow a little. I got a glimpse of the vibrant woman she must have been before she slid into severe suffering from a malfunctioning brain. I could see some tension leaving her body and relaxation flowing. That response gave me much hope.

Jack continued, "We've seen how God intervened in our lives and others' and pruned for a greater spiritual harvest. But this one has been difficult to endure." She nodded with teary eyes while Jack struggled to hold his tears back.

Joyce said, "I thought maybe if I worked harder, I could get better. I attempted to turn my negative feelings into positive experiences and I looked for ways to change my emotional and physical difficulties by being more optimistic and cheerful. But I had no energy to keep myself motivated . . . I quit going to the gym . . . and everything else."

CRY OF THE SUFFERING

On the outside this CEO tried to put on a smile and perform effectively, but severe anxiety was overwhelming her. Life had become irritating and unbearable. Finally, she was forced to quit her job. She couldn't go out of the house. Her husband, in addition to working, was doing his best to keep her from sinking deeper!

Joyce reached for a tissue, wiped her tears, and slowly began talking. She described symptoms of hormonal imbalance such as hot flashes, anxiety, bloated abdomen, mood swings, and other symptoms. Her migraines were poorly controlled with prescription drugs. She had lost 24 pounds over two years. Joyce had become overly vulnerable to stress. She had a high level of cortisol in her blood, low to no sex drive, and had trouble falling asleep. Her vital signs: blood pressure was 158/86 mmHg, pulse 70 beats/minute; weight 128 pounds; height 5'8".

ON MEDICATIONS

Joyce's symptoms had begun about 10 years earlier and had slowly intensified. She had no prior history of allergies or surgeries. Her tests for Alzheimer's disease and other dementias were negative. She had been thoroughly evaluated by many physicians for her complaints and was offered various medications.

Diagnosed as suffering from anxiety, insomnia, hypertension, depression, and short-term memory loss she had taken Zoloft, Celexa, Prozac, Effexor, Paxil, Depakote, Seroquel, Procardia XL, Premphase and Ambien.

Joyce looked at her hand-written notes and said, "I have been experiencing irregular periods for about four years, with impaired short-term memory, depression, and high cholesterol, for which I took Lipitor. I did what doctors asked me to do. Except for offering various medications to try, I was told that my symptoms were 'normal for my age.'"

"I have to tell you," Joyce continued, "My feelings of sadness, helplessness, and fatigue only grew worse due to the undesirable side effects of the meds. I was either mostly sleepy or restless; I would get stomach pains, nausea, constipation, and drowsiness." She added, "I tried to go off the meds. You can't imagine the agony of withdrawal symptoms, the nervousness, anxiety, nausea, headaches, shaking, insomnia, and others."

I asked Joyce, "Do you have sisters or brothers? Tell me about them."

Joyce replied, "Yes, I have an older sister and a younger brother. My brother is in good health, very upbeat and works as an engineer for a utility company. Jack and Tim play piano and guitar and entertain the family. Thank God, they definitely have no depression."

"My sister has been married for 28 years. She also has been going through mood swings and depression. She also takes meds, prays, and the problems haven't disappeared. As soon as I get better, she wants to make an appointment to see you."

"How is your relationship with your parents?" I asked.

"We have a great relationship; I regularly converse with them," Joyce responded.

"Joyce, did your mother suffer mood swings or anything else during her menopausal years?" I asked. "Yes, she had some mild symptoms, and she took a few herbal supplements with hormone pills . . . for less than a year. She tells me that my problems are a lot worse."

DECLINE OF SPIRITUAL LIFE

As our session continued, Joyce paused for as moment and asked Jack, "Honey, I am feeling tired but I want to continue. Could you please fill in for me?"

Jack slowly started talking. "I know she had cut down on all her spiritual activities because she wasn't able to cope with life. She didn't have the energy to get up in the morning and get ready to attend Sunday church services or mid-week prayer meetings. She completely stopped going to the ladies' Bible study, meeting people, and other activities.

"She expressed feelings of guilt and anxiety. She would read the Bible aloud and listen to Christian music to distract herself from her sadness. Frequently she would repent of her sins and begged God to keep her faith strong and to keep her from becoming bitter."

Joyce added, "It was impossible to practice my favorite verse, found in Colossians 1:11, 'to be strengthened with God's power, to endure with patience and joy.'"

THE PAIN OF PRUNING

In one of the sessions, Joyce said, "Well, it became my daily prayer to ask the Lord to show me any major sin that was causing Him to discipline me. In my despair, I would give God certain deadlines to show me if He was still pruning me. I had released all my ambitions, passions, and worldly desires completely to Him. I would have long conversations with God, followed by apologies. But nothing gave me relief."

Let there be no doubt: It was not her unconfessed sin or unwillingness to yield to the work of the Holy Spirit that was causing her problems.

JOYCE'S TREATMENT AND RECOVERY

Joyce and Jack repeatedly insisted she be treated only through natural means because she was on hormone replacement therapy (HRT) made from the urine of pregnant horses. Readers may recall the large doses of synthetic hormones given to more than 80 million women, who, as a result, were at increased risk for breast cancer, stroke, and pulmonary embolism.

Initially, I gave Joyce L-Carnosine and a special woman's, nutritional supplement called "Petal Soft" to balance her hormones, plus homeopathic remedies to alleviate her immediate suffering.

I ordered laboratory studies, including a chemistry test, complete blood count; saliva and urine analyses for neurotransmitter levels[3] (including hormone levels); red pack cell mineral and toxic element assays; thyroid, liver, and lipid tests; and a bioelectrical acupuncture meridian analysis. Most people however, do not require such extensive laboratory tests.

These lab studies revealed high total cholesterol, low HDL (high density lipoprotein, the "good cholesterol") of only 31 milligrams per deciliter (dl), mildly elevated blood sugar, very low IGF-1 (an immunoactive protein); elevated cortisol (a stress hormone), elevated estrogen (also a stress hormone, as well as a pivotal female sex hormone), and depleted levels of other hormones—progesterone, testosterone, and DHEA (dehydroepiandrosterone, the most abundant hormone in both sexes, a precursor of several other hormones).

Both depression and Hormone Replacement Therapy (HRT) could have lowered Joyce's DHEA. Anxiety was a major contributor to Joyce's high cortisol. HRT and anxiety drove up her estrogen level. Though her thyroid test was normal, her greatly

---

[3] Neurotransmitters are chemicals that transmit nerve impulses between brain cells.

elevated estrogen would suppress thyroid function, which in turn could contribute to her fatigue, as could low testosterone and depression. And remember, all these abnormalities of circulating hormones can stir up lots of trouble in the brain, as Joyce's misery clearly demonstrated.

After careful evaluation, I instructed Joyce and her husband in the basics of a balanced natural food diet; and I prescribed Joyce 50 milligrams (mg) of 7-keto DHEA daily, 50 mg of plant-derived progesterone daily in the morning, 0.1 milliliters (ml) micronized bioidentical testosterone gel (50 mg) daily, and nutritional supplements as follows: Nature's Hospital Complete Nutritional Mix; Brain Food, Neuro Complex, Heart Prolongevity (2 tablets), Anxiety/Stress Relief (chewable tablets); Natural Joint Integrity, Natural Sleep and 5-HTP (50 mg) 30 minutes before bedtime. She was also started on an exercise program designed just for her.

After three weeks, 3 Chromium with Cinnamon (2 capsules a day) was added to the above regimen to normalize her blood sugar and carbohydrate metabolism. By that time, her symptoms of brain chemical imbalance, multiple hormone insufficiency, anxiety, insomnia, and depression had diminished considerably.

Within five weeks, she claimed her brain fog had completely lifted. Her blood pressure had lowered to 128 over 76 (mmHg), a very healthy reading. Her glucose level was 88-96 milligrams per deciliter. Depression and all other symptoms had improved over 60 percent. Before the end of four months, she felt fully recovered, and she had been able to discontinue all pharmaceutical medications.

STAYING FOCUSED ON GOD

Four months and eight sessions later, Joyce returned to the clinic with a big, bright smile and a gift basket. This time she was accompanied by her husband and children. To make the story short, Joyce said, "My relationship with the Lord and my husband is blossoming. I can see once again God's beauty all around me. I am guilt- free, confident, and I have the peace of God in me. Entertaining people and talking to friends is not so frustrating."

"Many people now come and talk to me about their feelings of lack of joy, their mental, spiritual, and family struggles. I'm more aware of allowing the Holy Spirit to build in me Christ-like qualities and have Him minister the fruit of the Spirit to those who may need my service. Jesus healed people of mental and physical illness. I'm praying to God to give me continued health and strength so that I might be a blessing to hurting people."

Today, Joyce is learning everything she can about brain-related disorders and how to support suffering people. She is helping people find God's purpose in their problems and ways to resolve their difficulties and enable them to pursue Christlikeness in their lives. She once said, "I have no fear of failure, whatever may come. I feel the strength of my balanced brain, the power of the Holy Spirit, and the strength of God's Word."

A LIFE OF POWER

God has granted the author and his professional colleagues the privilege of witnessing numerous such transformations in the lives of Christians. Many Christians, once unable to break away from the burden of neurobiochemical imbalance or other brain disorders, spiritually just existing, living frustrated lives, have regained liveliness, mental clarity, godly enthusiasm, and a single-minded passion and power to follow the Lord with gusto.

A joy-filled life in the Holy Spirit is not only for a few of the spiritually elite. God has promised this relationship to every believer who would move beyond mediocrity. The Holy Spirit who empowered Joyce to victory is still in business!

So now you have a glimpse of how lives can be transformed with the right help. Thus, by God's grace, one can be instrumental in restoring people's health, for God's glory, by allowing the Holy Spirit to equip them to face the challenges of everyday life.

CHOOSING TO FINE-TUNE FOR POWER

By choosing to balance your brain and mind, you can facilitate the work of the Holy Spirit in your life. Some readers may find it more comfortable to be with people or professional therapists who empower deficits rather than challenge to transform deficits into strengths. But such associations make it easy to protect and defend your human weaknesses. Rather, we must focus on those goals which will make us more yielding to the Holy Spirit. For example: determine to make conscious lifestyle, food, and beverage choices that are best for your body and brain. This will boost your energy and joy in the Holy Spirit. Surround yourself with people who hunger for the Word of God. Develop a network of personal, spiritually hungry friends. Acknowledge the priceless value of prayer, fellowship, breaking of bread, biblical teaching, music, giving, and unconditional love. List your goals on paper and focus on accomplishing them, reinforced with God's strength.

Note: The term "fine-tuning the brain," brain balancing, brain change, brain power, mind transformation, and similar variants are used interchangeably throughout the book.

FOR REFLECTION

I am the true Vine, and My Father is the Vinedresser.
He cuts off every branch in Me that does not bear fruit.
He trims every branch for more fruit.

—John 15:1-2

Every trial can be viewed as a trial of faith to bring forth praise, honor, glory, and much enduring fruit (2 Corinthians 1:4; I Peter 1:7; John 15:2, 5, 16). Joyce's response to her struggles and suffering enabled her and those who cared for her "to work together for the good," that is, to make her more like Jesus Christ (Romans 8:28; John 1:3, cf. 2 Corinthians 1:5; Philippians 3:10).

Rather than blaming God or rebelling against Him, she was able to cooperate by faith and obedience. After her health was restored, her deepened compassion for others in trouble demonstrated the truth that wounded servants in the body of Christ often make better healers.

In Joyce's case, with patience and support, she was somehow able to hang onto the Lord until relief arrived in God's sovereign timing (Isaiah 49:8). If she hadn't received help, her condition might have worsened, resulting in despair and physical and spiritual deterioration. She might not have been able to yield to the Vinedresser's pruning or to fully comprehend the practical issue of surrendering her all to the Lord.

Have you seen such people? If you have, you may be able to help those individuals or families. How joyful it is to see the life of a fruitful Christian . . . a fruitful family . . . a fruitful church.

SERVANTS OF JESUS CHRIST

Taking decisive action to correct brain and hormonal dysfunction helped Joyce to change her brain imbalance, reduce stress, and resume vibrant living. In her case, identifying the cause of her illness required professional help. But in less severe cases, caring laymen, armed with knowledge, can be of great service to their suffering fellow man.

Helping people participate in tuning their brains, in combination with the supernatural work of God, often results in transformations of the lives of believers and non-believers. Sometimes such transformations are beyond what science, medicine, or "religion" can fully comprehend or explain (Psalm 40:5; 1 Corinthians 6:19, 20; 1 John 4:13), but they happen every day. You can share the beauty of the Lord Jesus with all His compassion and purity. Being filled with the Holy Spirit moment by moment and having a passionate personal relationship with God are paramount to being true servants of Jesus Christ. "For it is God who changes your mind and brain in you to enable you to act according to His good purpose" (Philippians 2:13).

How often have you seen humble servants receive the accolade of the crowd? In fact, true servants of Lord Jesus know that human recognition is dangerous! They listen to the voice of the Holy Spirit. "So if you eat, drink, or do anything else, do all to give God glory" (1 Corinthians 10:31).

Discussion Questions

1. How can you comfort and care for someone today? Read Ephesians 4:32 and 5:1–2. Identify a "neighbor" in your life. Take some recorded music and a meal and go worship with him or her. Worship with music can generate positive feelings and inhibit negative thoughts

and feelings. God will cover you with His power (1 Peter 1:5). He's not limited by your limitations (Ephesians 3:20). Go ahead, do it and share in the miracle of healing effects!

Answer:

2. Are you aware that changing hormone levels and severe premenstrual syndromes can occur many years before menopause? Are you aware this condition can interfere with spirituality? Also, many mothers become depressed during the first six months after the birth of a child. (Post-partum depression.) How can you help?

Answer:

3. Did treating Joyce's problems require one, two, or any of the following programs?

	YES	NO
a. Hormonal balancing?	___	___
b. Neurophysiological (brain) balancing?	___	___
c. Understanding drives and motivation (mind)?	___	___
d. Right use of the Bible?	___	___
e. Nutritional understanding?	___	___
f. Work of the Holy Spirit?	___	___
g. Love?	___	___

4. What do you think about traditional medicine slowly integrating a variety of alternative healing forms? How may this influence your spirituality?

Answer:

5. Are you a fruit-bearing Christian? Is your family bearing fruit? Is your church bearing fruit? Is your Christian business or work in the world bearing fruit? If not, why not?

Answer:

Chapter Two

Fine-Tuning Your Brain for Power: An Introduction

W hat exactly appears in your mind's eye when you think of fine-tuning your brain for power to ultimately become more like Christ? Does your mental picture line up with God's mental picture? Does your internal mental picture of the life and work of Christ appear as vivid as reality or does it appear faint, foggy, or nonexistent? The Bible asserts that through the indwelling Holy Spirit, believers, who individually and collectively constitute the body of Christ, comprehend, develop, and practice many and varied forms of the power of Christ (John 13:34; Ephesians 3:16–20; Philippians 4:7). Fine-tuning is the alignment of our lives to the life of the Lord Jesus Christ. This concept in the Bible involves the merging of the mind and matter, spirit and body, subject and object. Mary's miraculous conception by the Holy Spirit is viewed as union of the body, mind, and Spirit of God (Matthew 1:20). Researchers from various disciplines think that groups of complex "mirror neurons" may be involved in the process of imitation in the brain. Mirror neurons fire in our brains when we perform physical actions, visualize, observe other people, and internalize the observation in our brains. The point here is that as we read God's Word, the Holy Spirit holds up a mirror before us to show us how God sees us and how much adjustment is needed to reflect Christ-likeness. James writes, "The one who listens to the Word and does nothing is like a man who looks at his face in a mirror and right away forgets what he looks like" (James 1:23–24).

Does your brain need power to eagerly crave spiritual milk or meat (1 Peter 2:2)? Would your aspirations to achieve purity of mind and heart be furthered by spiritually empowering your brain (John 15:3)? Would you like to enjoy and celebrate your relationship with God by empowering your brain? Do spiritual things excite you or do you experience them as bland (Revelation 3:16)? Do you realize that a Bible-based brain tune-up is essential to empower you to reflect the character, nature, and life of Christ in you? Are you ready to empower your brain to fill your mind with the things of heaven so the "gates of hell" will not prevail against you (Matthew 16:19–23)? Embrace Christ-likeness!

INJURED BRAIN VS. INJURED MIND

Ironically, when we are physically injured, we seek help and often do not question the validity or appropriateness of the help we receive. When it comes to spiritual suffering due to brain deficits or chemical imbalances, the Church of Jesus Christ often lacks correct biblical information about the brain and its numerous functions, resulting in an unfavorable atmosphere in which believers cannot safely share their mental pain. We tend to ignore or only superficially address the issues.

Then, too, many followers of Christ frequently resist the fine-tuning of the Holy Spirit in our lives. Oh, we hear and know the "theological language" of "becoming more like Christ," all right. But we don't often allow our total person to fully relish the Holy Spirit's amazing adjustments. Retune your mind and conscience to God's Word and to the priorities He has reserved for your life. Pursue the freedom and power the Holy Spirit desires to give us by balancing the brain to generate spiritual growth. What a life!

CLARIFYING "FINE-TUNING" OR BRAIN POWER

When I define "fine-tuning" or brain power, I mean "repairing brain cells," "changing the environment to influence the brain chemistry," "putting our thinking back into a biblical balance," "experiencing the process of repentance," "experiencing the spiritual power of the brain in the process of transformation," "renewal through restoring optimal brain power to become more like Christ," "conforming to the image of the Lord Jesus," "developing a Christ-like mind-set," and so on. The final "aha" of recognizing the reality of true brain power comes only when we experience the life of Christ. It's like the difference between reading a gourmet recipe and actually savoring the food (Proverbs 20:30; Deuteronomy 12:2; James 1:22).

It is the work of the full trinity in the lives of willing people. It is God's plan for every non-believer and believer. It is a call you gladly receive to live for God. This begins with the process of merging with the breathtaking life of Christ, individually customized for our fragile lives.

This transformation embodies the spiritual, neuro-bio-psycho-electro-chemical activities which occur in the brain, mind, will, conscience, self, spirit, soul, and body of those who voluntarily yield their lives to God. It is a life separated from the unholy and set apart for God's service as citizens of heaven. To be a citizen of heaven means allowing God's rule or the life of Christ into every area of our lives. We are earthly people;

yet throughout our spiritual experience there is the ineffable connectedness, making us heavenly citizens. It's a partnership with the Holy Spirit in which the believer allows him or her to see the way the body-brain-mind influences his growth in Christ-likeness.

In fact, the work of the Holy Spirit cannot be reduced to just brain tissue. It is more than our 100 billion brain cells and their molecules. Fine-tuning is a dynamic process in which the Holy Spirit dwells within each believer, giving new life, instruction, wisdom, and spiritual power while transforming us into the image of Jesus Christ (Romans 8). A balanced brain is essential to being a "balanced believer." An imbalance of any of brain chemical can affect our actions, emotions, feelings [are feelings different from emotions?] and moods, our joys, and everything in life. One day we may feel spiritually motivated, joyous, and strong; the next day we may become arrogant, angry, moody, sad, anxious, or insensitive.

It is a way of life you joyously accept to follow to become like Jesus Christ. The biblical view of this life is neither one that forces us to do "more stuff" nor one that restrains us in the prison of cold legalism. It's a path of blessings, mixed with sufferings, and freedom, propelling you toward becoming the loving person God intended you to be. Fine-tuning shows how much you need God. It produces Christ-like character, purifies your life, and builds spiritual maturity. You'll have a smile on your face and power in your step.

It is a path of intense *agape,* Christ's kind of love. As Christ continues to spiritually form in us through the Holy Spirit (like a baby being formed in a mother's womb), we will become an endless source of love and bear other fruits of the Spirit.

So how do you fine-tune your brain for power? This awe-inspiring pursuit of Christ-likeness through fine-tuning your brain depends on many things: the "new birth experience"; individual genes; the formation and function of your brain from conception; the correct nerve cell connections and neurotransmitters generating and processing, and the integration of thought, sensation, emotion, will, impulse, conscience, and so on.

But if our brains suffer from structural abnormalities of the nerve cells or biochemical imbalances—for example: unhealthy nerve cell connections or depleted serotonin, dopamine, or norepinephrine levels—we may experience all kinds of problems: spiritual, cognitive, emotional, and social.

The process of transformation (growth) by the renewing of the mind also takes patience. It's a work-in-progress. Paul wrote, "be transformed" in the present imperative tense, meaning "keep on being transformed" (Romans 12:2; Ephesians 4:22–23).

It is God's plan for each of us, no matter what our level of neurological sophistication. Brain tuning for spiritual transformation is not an option. Rather it is an inseparable art of developing the life of Christ in us. Christ-like transformation occurs only when every part of a believer's total being is "made new" by fully and continually yielding to the control of the Holy Spirit to manifest the fruit of the Spirit (Ephesians 5:18; Colossians 3:15; Galatians 5:22–23).

THE ULTIMATE GOAL

The ultimate goal and the grand purpose of brain power are to become like Christ. Several words are used in Scripture to portray the beautiful outcome of fine-tuning. "The pure heart," "the pure mind," and "the mind of Christ" serve as images to illuminate many important functions of fine-tuning and brain power. David the King prayed, "Create dynamically pure thinking and desires in my body. Give me a new spirit that follows you faithfully" (Psalm 51:10). In the eighth chapter of Romans, the apostle Paul, in presenting this tremendous message he had been called by God to teach of being transformed in our minds by the Holy Spirit, wrote: "But the mind (Greek *Phronema*) controlled by the Spirit generates eternal life and peace" (Romans 8:6; cf. 5:1). The Holy Spirit will help you custom design an approach that will enable you to hear God speaking to you to fine-tune your brain. It also is a group project as you'll see in Chapter Five.[4]

Discussion Questions:

1. Do you believe that our transformation into Christlikeness is tied to brain balancing, neurotransmitter balance, or brain power?
   Here's one answer: Imagine you are listening to a favorite music composition on your portable CD-player. You are totally absorbed in the song when it starts playing slower and becomes distorted. The batteries have run down. You can no longer enjoy your music until you recharge the batteries.

2. Can you identify your spiritual, social, mental, physical, chemical, and characterological deficits that are direct expressions of brain imbalance or lack of brain power?

Answer:

3. Do you see how low or high neurotransmitter levels or defective genes can send incorrect or correct signals to neurons (nerve cells)?

Answer:

---

[4] Bible references for the above statements: Ezekiel 36:26; John 3:6, 14–17; Romans 8:1; 12:1,2; 1 Corinthians 6:19; Ephesians 1:11; Colossians 3: 5–12; Galatians 4:6.

4. Are you interested in fine-tuning your brain's biochemistry to optimize your spiritual vibrancy?

Answer:

Chapter Three

All of Us Need
Brain-Tuning for Mind Power

So are you convinced that all of us need brain-tuning for mind power? Let us face facts: most of us do not feel perfect—at least not all the time. Even the wisest, cognitively strongest among us, have times we don't feel fully competent or can't see the way forward nor do we have the right answers.

Every person's brain is unique and functions with some degree of imbalance from birth. Even when provided with an ideal environment, factors such as chronic stress, diet, genetic heritage, neurological imperfections, or imbalance of neurotransmitters or other molecules upon which normal brain functions depend can cloud our minds.

The Bible teaches that as a result of Adam's sin, our personalities are out of balance, and we all have inherited a level of brain, mind, body, and spirit dysfunction. Our ability to enjoy the presence and fellowship of God has been disrupted. Spiritual blindness has gradually engulfed our minds (2 Timothy 3:7). Sound extreme? The apostle Paul explained, "What the mind (Greek *Phronema*) of a sinful person thinks leads to physical and spiritual death. But the person whose mind is controlled by the Spirit generates life and peace" (Romans 8:6).

Some of us may not accept or know that we suffer an imbalance because the imbalance has become so much a part of us that we believe it is simply the way the Christian life is.

Imagine . . . the cell functions or chemicals in our delicate brains go out of balance, causing mental, spiritual, social, and emotional disharmony we lose all perspective! We may lose the ability to examine ourselves honestly, react biblically to environmental stimuli, or to distinguish between Christ-like and non-Christ-like actions on our own due to Adam's sin, generational effects of sin, and our own sin. The apostle Paul summarizes the dreadful condition of our fallen nature: we gravitate toward pride, disobedience, and self-rule (Ephesians 2:1–2; Colossians 1:13–14).

In short, the Bible says: When such highly complex brain functions are controlled by the sinful nature, it is difficult for the Holy Spirit to fill us and give us Christ-like qualities such as love, joy, peace, patience, kindness, goodness, faithfulness, gentleness, and self-control (Galatians 5:22-23, Ephesians 3:16), unless a person repents. Repentance means making a complete turnaround away from sin and experiencing transformation by the Holy Spirit.

TUNING FOR POWER BEGINS WITH SPIRITUAL BIRTH FOR ALL

The *first* brain-tuning can be viewed as salvation from our sins. It begins when you repent and experience by faith a total transformation from a natural to a spiritual person (Hebrews 11:6). Repentance literally means "a change of directions" (Luke 15:17–18).

In 1 Corinthians 2:14–16b, the Apostle Paul wrote: "Since some people don't have the Holy Spirit, they wouldn't and couldn't understand the things that come from the Spirit of God. Everyone who has the Spirit and is guided by Him is able to evaluate and apply all things the Spirit reveals . . . Spiritual people can understand these things, for they have the mind of Christ" (cf. v. 10; 4:3–5; Philippians 2:5–8).

The non-Bible-believing neuroscientists may, with confidence, claim to gain correct knowledge about the brain, mind, conscience, soul, spirit, and spirituality. But Bible-believing scientists should be able to explore with greater confidence the relationship between the physical brain and true spirituality simply because the Bible sheds a vast array of light on many of the complex issues pertaining to the body, mind, and the work of the Holy Spirit.

JESUS TEACHES ABOUT PHYSICAL AND SPIRITUAL LIFE

To assist believers in comprehending their own process of fine-tuning for power, Jesus presented distinct earthly analogies to further explain the many abstruse spiritual matters such as the trinity, the incarnation, faith, salvation, Jesus' coming in glory, and the like. For example, He beautifully and harmoniously linked our temporary physical human home and our spiritual eternal home. He emphasized that there are two realms: one is of fallen humans, and the other is of those who are born of the Spirit of God. This great transformation from one life to the other is initiated when one accepts Christ as Savior and Lord by faith. This fine-tuning is a supernatural gift of God's grace. Listen: God says He wants to "accomplish a new thing" for you (Isaiah 43:19).

THE RAPTUROUS GOD-MAN UNION

If you're not ready for the second level of fine-tuning, you'll miss the great relationship God offers you. Jesus also distinctly clarifies the invisible, yet discernable, work of the "Spirit" by employing the Greek word, *pneuma*. *Pneuma* is used to mean both physical "wind" or "breath" and the "Spirit" of God to connect the spiritual and physical life (John. 3:8, cf. John 20:22; Matthew 13:11). Jesus spoke to Nicodemus, a prominent lawyer and teacher, who, however, did not understand the spiritual dynamics of transformation, i.e., the reality of "being born again" (John 3:3). Combining various themes in His answer, Jesus seems to be explaining that all our perceptions are subjective by their nature, even those of material reality, and the human mind is incapable of separating spiritual mysteries from the fallen body (flesh) without divine transformation. His discourse with Nicodemus makes a strong case that there is more to mere human material existence and that our minds are capable of experiencing God's majestic realities of the Kingdom of God (Colossians. 1:13). From Jesus' teaching we learn that this physical world and the person who has not experienced the supernatural birth are slowly disintegrating and facing eventual destruction. This course can only be reversed when the Spirit of Christ enters a person.

In a spiritual, climactic crescendo, the Lord Jesus likened this experience to being born again (John 3:3, cf. Matthew 18:3). The term "born again" (Greek *Anothen*) literally means "born from above"; that is, being born spiritually through the Spirit of God because it is He who bestows the power on us to become children of God (Greek. *Ginomai*). God's Spirit now dwells in His children who have experienced supernatural new birth. The Bible teaches that "whenever anyone is in Christ, he is a new creation"; "But anyone who joins the Lord in spiritual union, becomes one with Him" (2 Corinthians 5:17; Romans

8:9; 1 Corinthians 6:17; 3:16).[5] This means we fully accept that Christ died for our sins and rose from the dead. Only the blood of the holy, sinless Son of God is capable of paying the penalty for our sins (Hebrews 9:22). Through His sacrifice, He paid for our sins and rescued us from eternal death. This entire process is God's logical plan for each of us to know God personally. That gives us godly confidence! In fact, He is waiting to show you favor. Change your will and make a move so He can perform a miracle in your life (Revelation 21:5). Are you ready?

Discussion Questions

1. Do you know God personally?

Answer:

2. Do you have a family history of inherited mental imbalance that discourages you from spiritual activities?

Answer:

3. Are you fine-tuning your brain to become more like Christ?

Answer:

4. Do you have any difficulties relating to an invisible God? If so, how do you resolve them?

Answer:

---

[5] The linking of the spiritual, neurobiological and other aspects of the new birth experience will appear in Volume 3.

Chapter Four

An Explanation of the Neurobiological Process of Transformation

I am going to attempt a brief explanation of this complex process (also see picture "stage three" in the middle section of the book). This process, from the time you receive the gospel message to finally allowing Christ to enter into our lives by faith, is controlled by infinitely complex, elaborate, and subtle interactions between the brain-mind and the Holy Spirit (Romans 8:9,15). This interaction involves genes and specific nutrients activating neurological and hormonal signals, bioenergetic activation or transformation of neurons, conscience, and other less well known factors.

The *Holy Spirit* is the invisible spiritual person directing this transformative process. A *neuron* (brain cell) is a highly specialized cell, consisting of a cell body. From one end of it extends many dendrite fibers. These receive information from other neurons. From the other end of the cell body extends an axon which is a flexible tube-like structure through which chemical messengers travel.

Within a neuron a bioelectrical impulse from other neurons travels toward the cell body through the dendrites. These impulses pass through the cell body and exit through the insulated long axon fiber. Neurons do not touch one another; they dispatch their messengers across tiny fluid-filled gaps called *synapses*. An electrical impulse from an axon enters the synapse and triggers the release of neurotransmitters which convey the impulse to the dendrites of adjacent neuron(s). The neurotransmitters bind to protein channels in the dendrites of the receiving neuron.[6]

More than one hundred billion neurons in the brain—by means of the neurotransmitters, synapses, neurohormones and neuromodulators—process, store and transmit an endless stream of data about Christ to every cell in the body. The integrated, complex process of repeatedly utilizing newly established neural pathways produce further changes in the brain, through the will and mind (Romans 12:2; Ephesians 4:23), resulting in behavior reflecting the lifestyle of Jesus Christ. These neurobiological changes and the resulting behavioral transformation are not the result of mere *'operant conditioning'*[7] rather, they involve the transforming work of the Spirit of God.

In order to understand the basic relationship between the brain and the new birth experience, I have analyzed the brain waves of people with normal brain structure before, during, and after the "born again" experience. There is a correlation between certain brain wave states and complete or partial surrender to the Lord Jesus Christ. In most instances the physical

---

[6] The channels allow a small flow of charged molecules (ions) to absorb some of the voltage from the recipient neuron. Scientists believe that this temporary strengthening of the synapse is the basis for short-term memory. Repeated synaptic firing at high frequency becomes the basis for long-term memories.

[7] Originally, the term *operant conditioning* meant behaviors being trained to result in a series of learned responses.

and emotional manifestation observed in those who appear to completely surrender, suggest a state of profound tranquility. Those who prayed the "salvation prayer" without deep conviction and trust, i.e. those who were unable to fully surrender with childlike trust (Matthew 18:4) reached only a partial state of brain wave tranquility. In the ensuing years, most of those who completely surrendered seemed to make consistent progress in their spiritual walk. Those who achieved only a partial state of cerebral tranquility showed only a partial surrender in their commitment to the Lord Jesus Christ, as reflected in their partially changed lifestyles, with retention of bad habits or a tendency to lapse into spiritual decline.

Although the process of Christ-like formation is one of progressively casting off sinful habits and growing in joy and virtue, complete surrender of the will through faith at the "new birth" experience seems to result in a quantum leap of spiritual mind transformation. That transformation impels the believer forward through creating a desire for the things of heaven.

However, a dramatic conversion experience may not be essential. Everyone's journey is unique. He who progresses along quietly on the Christian path just as surely may achieve Christ-likeness. Whether the pilgrim has a sudden transformational experience or an agonizingly slow "born-again" experience, the magnetism of God's love, once we have had a taste of it, draws us irresistibly toward Christ-likeness. Whether gradual or sudden, the process of transforming the mind has a special moment in time like the birth of a baby.

It should also be noted that some individuals engage in Christian spiritual activities but do not allow their wills to surrender to the intervention of the Holy Spirit. Therefore, neuroanatomical changes may not occur because the Holy Spirit is not able to change the individual's thinking based on the prior history of encoding. It is possible that some of these individuals have personality disorders or other mental or emotional problems due to their brains being out of sync. Their brain's electrical function as it processes biochemicals in various locations may have a surplus or deficiency preventing biblical insight from entering into their mind to accomplish a life-changing relationship with Jesus Christ.

These neurobiological insights into Christian transformation are only preliminary; they need to be confirmed by further experiments, observations, and activation studies (studies of brain images obtained while people engage in specific spiritual decision-making processes).

THE HOLY SPIRIT'S ENCODING OF THE BRAIN

Numerous biblical passages, some cited in this volume, suggest that seeking a living Creator-God is hardwired into the human brain.

It is important to recognize the scriptural teaching that at spiritual rebirth one must completely surrender to the Holy Spirit's work of encoding[8] into the mind the capacity to emulate Christ Jesus. Spiritually, it is an experience of being ushered into a fulfilling realm of pure, heavenly, joyful consciousness. This awakening of the believer is reflected in the release of many neurotransmitters that travel throughout the brain sending messages and activating hormones. These in turn influence nerves and organs throughout the body. Due to these biological processes and spiritual activities, the believer is able to perceive, assess, and judge his life based on the Scriptures.

---

[8] Making of memories in the human brain is still shrouded in mystery. Yes, neuroscientists have attempted to understand memory storing and networking using a variety of animals. But such questions as how genes direct memory formation or why genes turn on to transcribe DNA, etc., are slowly being understood.

It is a revolutionary, powerful human experience involving the visual images of a sinless Christ dying in the place of the guilty. Without being able to totally admit that the Bible is true—and believe fully in your heart that Jesus lived here on earth, died and rose again—it is impossible for the explosive images to be encoded by the entire brain and body (Romans 8:2,9; 12:2). These spiritual realities are distributed throughout the brain, beginning the process of conformity to Christ-likeness.

> If you confess with your mouth, "Jesus is Lord," and believe in your whole being that God raised Him from the dead, then you will be saved. For in your heart you believe and are made right with God. By your confession you are saved.
>
> —Romans 10:9, 10

> God is able to do far more than we could ever ask for or imagine. He does everything by His power that is working in us.
>
> —Ephesians. 3:20

Discussion Questions

1. How much do you recall of the time in your life when the Holy Spirit revealed the glory of God and the love of Christ, leading to your decision to make a complete turnaround?

Answer:

2. Were you thoroughly convinced of your sin and the need for an intense desire to follow the Lord Jesus?

Answer:

3. Do you perceive ongoing growth toward Christ-like-ness since your acceptance of Christ?

Answer:

4. How may each of the images Paul presents in Colossians 2:7—rooted, built-up, growing strong, and overflowing relate to the function of the brain and your spiritual growth?

Answer:

5. Wonders of the brain: How do activities in different neurons generate well-coordinated waves in the brain, producing seemingly incalculable three-dimensional images? How do electrical and chemical impulses transform into thought, visual image, feeling, conscience, and influence the inner spiritual person? Part of the answer lies in the explanation Jesus gave to Nicodemus. "The blowing of the wind is invisible. You hear the sound of it, but cannot tell where it comes from and where it goes. It is the same with everyone who is born of the Spirit" (John 3:8). How can we unravel the true mysteries of the mind without the knowledge the Creator has provided in the Bible?

Chapter Five

God's Golden Rule . . .
Brain-Tuning and
Mind Power Require
a Supportive Community

OUR SOCIAL BRAIN

It's not surprising that the Holy Spirit revealed to Paul in-depth knowledge about the brain-mind design, structure, and functions germane to the dynamics of the Christian community. They are found in the more than 55 different "one another" injunctions in the New Testament.

As you read this chapter, bear in mind that the body of Christ is meant to function very much like a healthy human brain and nervous system. Recent findings in neuroscience indicate the indispensability of brain neurons communicating with one another based on mutual stimulation. Brain cells strive to connect with one another and thrive on harmonious relationships. Consider the enormously complex ways in which neural pathways cross the midline as they enter the brain. Sensory and motor functions for the right side of the body are controlled and processed in the left side of the brain and sensory and motor function for the left side of the body are controlled and processed in the right side of the brain. In the vast majority of nearly seven billion souls on our planet, all this complicated crossing over and interconnecting is accomplished without error, resulting in a smooth and coordinated functioning of each person. This masterpiece of God's handiwork serves as a paradigm of harmony and interconnectedness of the spiritual and social body of Christ.

A study by the Center for Disease Control and Prevention found that having plenty of social support is linked to a better quality of life and mental health. Listen to the words of Jesus about building valuable relationships: "In all things, treat others as you would wish them to treat you" (Matthew 7:12). "Anything you did for one of the least important brothers of mine, you did for me" (Matthew 25:40 cf., Matthew 22:37–39; See also 1 Corinthians 12:18–21). "Anyone who accepts someone I send accepts me" (John 13:20a). The apostle Paul expressed a similar thought to the Galatians: "You were invited to a life of freedom, my brothers and sisters! Don't turn away from your freedom to choose a destructive lifestyle. Instead, serve one another in love—as if you were cheerfully serving the Lord and not people" (Galatians 5:13; Ephesians 6:7b). And again, examine Hebrews 10:24, "Consider how we can rally love for one another and do good." Understand this richly rewarding scriptural truth: there are no limitations in God's plan to reward you for showing love to others. The enemy cannot stop God from blessing you for your love of others.

Jesus came to us to establish a social milieu based on free will, love, and decency for all. God, who created Adam in His image, concluded, "It is not good for man to be alone" (Genesis 2:18a, 27). Even Jesus needed the support of His parents, other people and angels (Mark 1:13). The Apostle Paul reached out for help and received it on many occasions. When we are walking in the Spirit, not only will we be sensitive to His guidance about our lives, but we will be sensitive to whomever he sends our way.

HUMANS ARE CREATED TO LIVE AND WORK WITH ONE ANOTHER

Being made in God's likeness, most of us are born with powerful social instincts. The Bible portrays God as a loving Person who thinks, feels, and identifies with people. His essential nature is love. We need God's unimaginably sweet love and he longs to receive love from his children. This is planned by God. The Christian life is not just our own private business to be lived in isolation. God places a high value on building vibrant relationships in the body of Christ. If you try to live the Christian life alone, in most cases, you are setting yourself a very difficult course. God is more interested in each of us becoming more like Christ as we live together, taking time to lift up one another, bind the wounded, and encourage one another as we journey along. That's one more reason to be connected and committed to a Bible-believing, Christ-centered body of Christ.

The apostle Paul describes beautifully in the third chapter of Ephesians the way in which God has established a wonderful Spirit-based social culture among the created and redeemed. We all belong to the family of God. God wants His children to learn the basic principles of getting along with one another and to enjoy the family of God. If you have not enjoyed the best experience in the Christian community, you will not be able to impart good experiences to those you meet. Once you have had a sweet glimpse of what the King of the universe has prepared in His royal palace for His children, nothing else will satisfy. At first glance, people in general, and a large percentage of believers seem basically self-centered. So we must take the initiative to change all that by sincerely demonstrating the self-sacrificing love of Christ. Also, reach out for help when in need and trust God to lead you to those who can help you. Thus we may lay the biblical groundwork for building Christ-like relationships (1 Corinthians 13; Ephesians 5:17).

MAJESTIC HONOR BESTOWED

After the new birth experience, God expects all believers to share their life together in the family of God (Acts 2:42). The purpose of this majestic honor bestowed on every believer is to follow God in an endless journey of single-minded passionate romance, to be winners in becoming like Christ. Christ-likeness takes place in the context of the family of God (1 John 3:14–16). We are families with the greatest commandment: "to love God wholeheartedly and to love your neighbor as yourself" (Matthew 22: 34–40; Mark 12:28–33; Luke 10:27). But pay attention: did you notice that the greatest commandment never appears by itself? Paul says, love must be pure and we must love each other deeply. Paul added that we are to honor others more than yourself with brotherly love (Romans 12:9, 10).

Is your personality predisposed to feeling threatened by somebody else's superior spiritual gifts or talents? If so, you need to surrender your jealousy and insecurity to God and pray for transformation. Such traits are essentially bad habits of ego nature. They can be changed by the work of the Holy Spirit, by persistent, vigilant application of willpower, and by deliberately transmuting the small-minded emotion of jealousy to the expansive feeling of admiration and pleasure in another's fine qualities. Supplementation to correct nutritional deficiencies and restore dynamic balance in the brain may significantly facilitate such efforts.

Paul exhorts believers to "Help others also while you help yourselves" (Philippians 2:4). Again Paul said "Find pleasure in honoring each other" (Romans 12:10). Our Lord Jesus gave one primary command to believers: "Love each other, just as I have loved you" (John 15:12). Jesus Christ is committed to empowering His children to build and maintain loving relationships. Caring for and nurturing each other is indispensable for growing in Christ-likeness. Involvement in the lives of others can boost your energy and build evangelism and discipleship skills. These can teach one how to manage stress better. Also involvement with other believers helps resolve some emotional conflicts, especially those acquired from childhood experience. Believers can help other believers cope with personal disputes, separation, loss, and transition to new and challenging social roles. When you see conflict in church, Bible study, or other situations, cultivate the skill of peacemaking.

No one needs to live a life of spiritual poverty and defeat. The plan of God for the Body of Christ inescapably involves the fellowship of the Holy Spirit: caring, sharing, and loving one another in the process of our spiritual growth. God can make a life of victory and holiness possible to every believer by practicing pure "agape" love that is honest and true (Romans 12:9-21; 1 Corinthians 13). It does not matter whether we are born poor or rich, have little or much education, suffer illnesses or are the picture of health; somehow, by faith, we can all participate in the Body of Christ. In the same way the paralyzed man caught the attention of Jesus (John 5:5). God can move someone to "carry you to Jesus." We are called upon to make ourselves fully available to follow Him, anywhere, anytime, and under any circumstance.

OPPORTUNITIES GOD PROVIDES
FOR COMMUNITY

Debilitating brain suffering may not be just a "thorn" in the flesh or seasonal "pruning" for some Christians because their pain and misery lasts a lifetime. That is a great weight to carry. So they are miserable, dissatisfied, unfulfilled, have no joy in the Lord, and are unable to enjoy praising, singing, and worshiping. It appears that their suffering never ends. As the apostle Paul beautifully wrote to the Roman believers, such people are opportunities God provides for the body of Christ to show *agape.* He said, "Keep receiving one another into our lives as Christ received us to the glory of God" (Romans. 15:7). In the same vein, Paul commanded, "Rejoice with those who rejoice; mourn with those who mourn" (Romans. 12:15).

We ought to learn to be receptive to mentally challenged children, brothers, and sisters, just as Christ received us. We ought to serve them. Offering hospitality as though you were serving Jesus Christ is its own reward. Sharing what you have encourages others because it demonstrates freedom from want and trust in God to meet personal needs (Romans. 12:13; 1 Peter. 4:9–10). Jesus' entire life was an example of love, kindness, and healing; and our mandate as Christians is to follow Him and strive for Christ-likeness. May our ministries be of service to those who are burdened with mental illness, pain, sorrow, and sickness.

In Chapter 10, you will have an opportunity to discover your brain needs and how to integrate physical, spiritual, neurological, psychological, nutritional, and social interventions to help yourself and others. When you are provided with an awareness of what the brain needs, and learn to free yourself from limiting brain disharmony, you can turn the shame and guilt of failure to triumph in the work of emulating Christ Jesus in your life.

"Do you not know that in a race, all runners run, but only one wins the prize? Run in such a way as to receive the prize" (1 Corinthians 9:24). Pray that you'll allow the Holy Spirit to transform your thinking to conform to His thinking about all members of the body of Christ as one family.

LOVE THOSE WITH BRAIN MALFUNCTIONS— IF THEY WILL LET YOU

For many Christians, when encountering new people or new places or situations, their hearts beat faster, their hands sweat and become cold, butterflies flutter in their stomach, and they cannot speak freely. These are signs of stress response. In one study 22-year-old people were given a PET scan imaging while they looked at the faces of strangers. In those classified as behaviorally inhibited by the age of two, their amygdalae—the center of fear conditioning in the brain—displayed increased activity. Children in the same age group who were evaluated to be extroverted, the amygdalae remained basically calm.

Usually fearfulness is associated with irregularities in the activity of the neurotransmitters dopamine and serotonin, accompanied by abnormally high levels of corticotrophin and cortisol—stress hormones. To reach some people, we need to go into their sometimes not-so-easy mental environment to make a difference. That means to patiently identify with their struggles. There is a vast number of brain-deficient Christians in the Body of Christ. They are often discouraged and believe nothing will help them. I have seen many such cases. These are people who are much more likely to drop out of church involvement, leading to spiritual and social isolation. That's where you can fill in the gap! Everybody is assigned to somebody in the Body of Christ. Refuse to be self-centered and

Fine Tuning The Brain Naturally

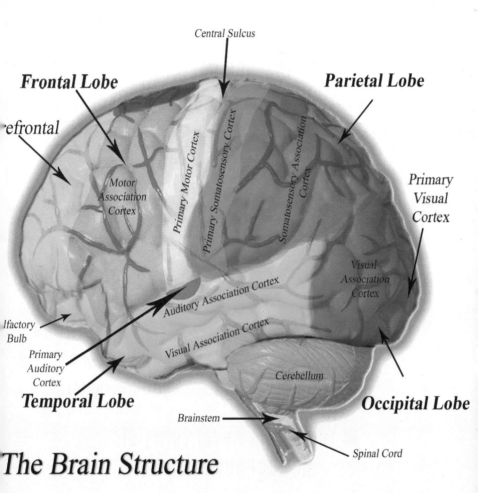

Central Sulcus

Frontal Lobe

Parietal Lobe

efrontal

Motor Association Cortex

Primary Motor Cortex

Primary Somatosensory Cortex

Somatosensory Association Cortex

Primary Visual Cortex

Visual Association Cortex

Auditory Association Cortex

lfactory Bulb

Visual Association Cortex

Primary Auditory Cortex

Cerebellum

Temporal Lobe

Brainstem

Occipital Lobe

Spinal Cord

The Brain Structure

Basic Brain Bytes

■ Cerebral cortex is the outermost layer of the brain. It measures about 1/8 inch in thickness. It is estimated that the neurons of one human cerebral cortex, if placed end to end and measured, would extend to 250,000 miles.

■ The average adult brain weighs about 3 pounds

■ Your brain began making, arranging, and wiring circuits in your mother's womb.

■ Your brain never turns off throughout your life

■ Electrical messages in neurons travel about 220 miles per hour. It translates to 32 feet per second

Basic Brain Bytes Cont.

■ Your brain processes a thought at the speed of 320 milliseconds, or about one third of a second

■ By the time you were born 100 billion neurons were already formed

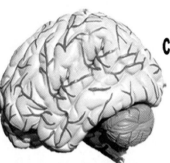

■The brain consumes about 30 percent of the body's energy

■ The human genome sequence is more than 99.9 percent the same in all people

■ Genes and brain chemistry influence our personality and total being. They are not wired together. But as you grow they continue to fire and make new connections. Throughout life you regenerate new neurons as your old neurons die away. Eventually as you age, glial cells, called support cells, grow new circuits compensating for losses

Fine Tuning The Brain Naturally

ONE NEURON

Dendrite ——→
(Nerve Fiber Arms)

Mitochondrion ——→ ←—— **Nucleus**

←—— **Cell Body**

Axon
(Nerve Fiber) ——————→

Myelin Sheath ——————→ ←—— **Schwann Cell**

Telodendria ——→ ←—— **Node of Ranvier**

Every child is born with over one hundred billion neurons.
These cells are the smallest components of our nervous system.
The nucleus houses the genetic material of the cell.
Every neuron transmits information via electrical current.

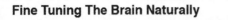

STAGE TWO

NEURON Transmission

Direction of Impulse Flow

Dendrite
(Nerve Fiber Arms)

Mitochondrion

Nucleus

Cell Body

Axon
(Nerve Fiber)

Myelin Sheath

Schwann Cell

Node of Ranvier

Axon Terminals

The passage of a nerve impulse starts at Dendrite and flows down the cell body to the Axon. The Axon terminals lie close to the Dendrites of neighboring Neurons. When the nerve impulses reach an Axon terminal it releases a chemical messenger (neurotransmitter) that crosses the synaptic gap. (See next diagram)

Neuron Transmission and Crossing the Gap

Direction of Impulse Flow

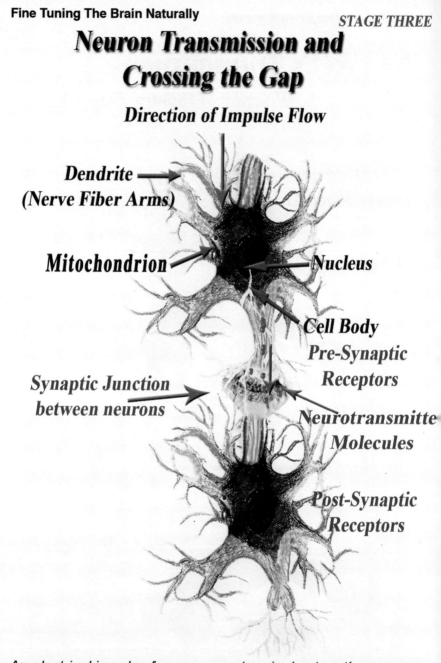

Dendrite
(Nerve Fiber Arms)

Mitochondrion

Nucleus

Cell Body
Pre-Synaptic
Receptors

Synaptic Junction
between neurons

Neurotransmitte
Molecules

Post-Synaptic
Receptors

An electrical impulse from an axon terminal enters the synapse and triggers the release of neurotransmitters into a synaptic junction (or gap) which conveys the impulse to the dendrites of adjacent neuron(s), down the axon and continues the cycle. The result of millions of cells communicating with each other electrically and chemically make up our behavior.

Degeneration of Myelin in Multiple Sclerosis

Healthy Myelin Sheaths

Absence of Myelin

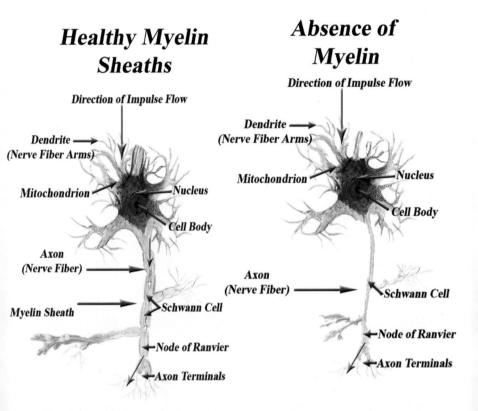

Myelin is a fatty substance that insulates and protects the axons of neurons. Myelin is necessary for proper transmission of signals for numerous functions.
In MS myelin disintegrates in the brain, spinal cord and the optic nerves producing scarring and plaques which results in various disorders.

Attention System

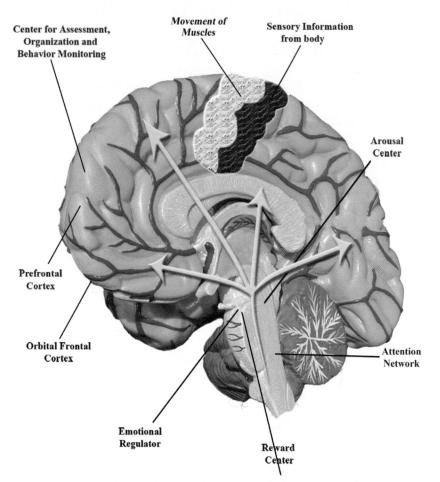

Center for Assessment,
Organization and
Behavior Monitoring

Movement of
Muscles

Sensory Information
from body

Arousal
Center

Prefrontal
Cortex

Orbital Frontal
Cortex

Attention
Network

Emotional
Regulator

Reward
Center

Many researchers have concluded that the frontal cortex alone is involved in deficits of attention. All of the drugs developed for the treatment of inattention (i.e. ADD and ADHD) target the frontal cortex enhancing levels of norepinephrine and dopamine by various mechanisms. However, various laboratory assays (such as measuring neurotransmitters or their metabolites in urine) and neuro-imaging studies strongly suggest that the entire brain participates to some degree in generating attention, inattention, distractibility and impulsivity. Proceeding from this evidence, it seems to be more sensible to address disorders of attention globally as a problem of the whole terrain of the brain rather than altering levels of one or two neurotransmitters in the frontal cortex with patent drugs -- all of which are toxic, carry the risk of potentially serious side effects, and are entirely lacking in curative capability. The preferred solution is comprehensive intervention aimed at restoring balance and promoting optimal functioning not only in the whole brain but in the whole organism. Thus modification of diet, lifestyle, habits and attitudes provides the foundation for more specifically directed interventions such as supplementation, neurofeedback, homeopathic treatment, and whatever other gentle therapies may be deemed necessary. The desired outcome is not just superior concentration but maximizing a person's potential so that he can fully participate in God's plan for him.

ALZHEIMER`S
The progressive and degenerative nature of the disease.

The progressive degeneration of brain tissue is characterized by the gradual spread of sticky neuritic plaques called beta amyloid and clumps of tangled fibers. The disease develops in the interior part of the brain beginning at the bottom and spreads to the cortex while atrophying the brain cells. As the disease spreads, cells stop communicating with one another.

Cerebral Cortex

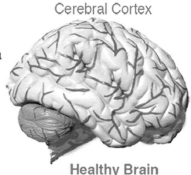

Healthy Brain

Stage 1 is characterized by progressive forgetfulness, lack of sleep, loss of short-term memory, increased anxiety, restlessness, severe mood swings, outbursts of anger, disorientation and loss of coordination may accompany depression. The Brain may begin to shrink in size and weight.

Stages 1 & 2

Disease Progression

In **Stage 2**, past memory may remain intact, immediate memory becomes elusive. The early signs of disorientation becomes a daily experience. Writing difficulties, distorted language and cognitive deficits take the victim further into a foggy world as the disease eats away healthy cells. The person is usually aware of this helpless predicament as brain cells die in greater numbers. In most cases, personality begins to rapidly deteriorate.

ALZHEIMER`S
The progressive and degenerative nature of the disease.

Stage 3

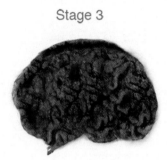

An Atrophied Alzheimer's Brain

In Stage 3, when the tangles and plaques infiltrate the cerebral cortex, cherished memories are lost. Memories of all kinds and capacity for abstract thought processes are lost. Personality and spirtuality are also destroyed as the brain dies away. Most people are unable to recognize God, spiritual realities, loved ones, themselves or most anything. Usuall delusions, hallucinations, passivity, sleeplessness or violent episodes m force many to require hospitalization or full-time nursing-home care services.

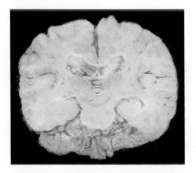

Slice of Normal Brain

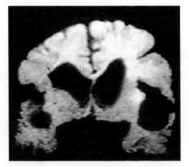

Slice of Alzheimer's Brain

Fine Tuning The Brain Naturally

ALZHEIMER`S
The progressive and degenerative nature of the disease.

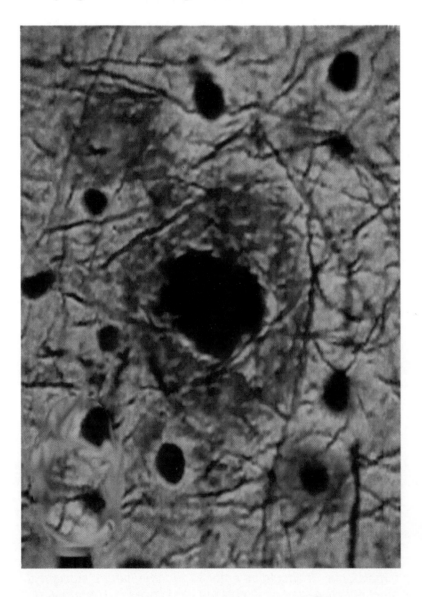

TANGLES, PLAQUES and HOLES in an Alzheimer's Brain

Light, Melatonin, the Biological Clock and Sleep

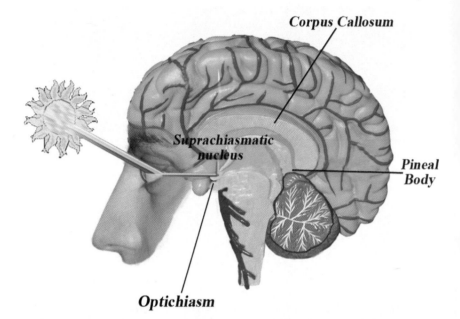

Corpus Callosum

Suprachiasmatic nucleus

Pineal Body

Optichiasm

Deep within the brain in the anterior hypothalamus lie two clusters, each made up of thousands of neurons called suprachiasmatic nuclei (SCN) which regulates the body's circadian rhythms. This is powered by the light that enters through the retina of the eye. When light strikes the retina, signals are generated and travel to the SCN via neural pathways called retinohypothalamic tract. Then the signals are reached by the SCN and processed and sent to a small number of certain hypothalamic cells but chiefly to the pineal gland which produces the hormone melatonin. Melatonin production begins with an inhibitory neurotransmitter, an amino acid, tryptophan. Then through a group of enzyme-catalyzed reactions, tryptophan is partially changed to 5-hydroxytryptophan (5HTP), which is connected in varying degrees to serotonin and melatonin. It should be emphasized that natural sunlight is the most effective way of stimulating this process. Therefore, get regular exposure to sunlight (safely) to promote restful sleep. Sunlight also has a beneficial effect on depression and many bodily functions.

resist going with the mundane flow! God desires to use you to be His hands and feet in supporting such people, even if it means sacrificing your time, resources, and yourself. Understand their mental status and find a way to be a source of blessing in their life. When you do, you will receive blessings multiplied now and in eternity. That's part of God's plan to mature you into Christ-likeness (Matthew 10:42).

But our Lord Jesus said, "Whatever you did for one of the least of these brothers of mine, you did for me" (Luke 10:16). "Carry one another's extreme difficulties. If you do, you will satisfy the law of Christ" (Galatians. 6:2).

The strongest argument for the uniqueness of Christians should not be based on exhaustive rules and regulations about spirituality that we struggle to observe without the power of Christ, but on the dynamic practical life of Jesus Christ that spontaneously emanates the sweet fragrance of His love and service from our lives (2 Corinthians 2:14 cf. Romans 8:18, 30; Colossians 1:24).

Discussion Questions

1. Do you think that social connectedness with members of God's family is important for your spiritual wellness?

Answer:

2. Do you physically contribute to the members of your church by being involved in church social activities perhaps even when you don't feel like it?

Answer:

3. At the age of sixty-three, Amy Carmichael fell into a pit in India. In pain and suffering, she continued to faithfully serve the people of India from her home in Dohnavur (Doe-nah-voor) (The author visited her orphanage in Southern India). Carmichael had a can-do attitude and exhibited joy in spite of her circumstance. Do you have a can-do attitude and joy about involvement with members of God's family?

Answer:

4. There is room for all races in God's present and future kingdom. Is there room for all kinds of people in your life? This biblical reality of hospitality and openness of heart and mind is marked for time and eternity and nothing can change it! Is your heart open to all, whatever the color of their skin?

Answer:

5. Would you like to call your church to find out what you can bring in the way of games, gifts, food, music, or something to make the social event extra special?

Answer:

6. Identify a list of potential problems associated with providing help for people with various brain disorders.

Answer:

Chapter Six

The Brain's Plasticity and Fine-Tuning

Brain plasticity means that the brain is flexible and able to change itself at any age throughout our lives. Neuroplasticity also refers to structural and functional changes in the formation and elimination of synapses, the connections between neurons. The overwhelming great message of the Bible from beginning to end is the miracle of mind and brain transformation. This flexibility makes salvation, Christ-likeness, and many changes in the brain possible. Of course, it is only in the past two decades that scientists have uncovered evidence of the brain's plasticity. So, in a nutshell, as mentioned in previous chapters, brain and body chemistry influence the mind, temperament, spirit, soul, will, conscience, and indeed one's entire being in a continuous feedback loop. It's important to remember that the brain's plasticity enables the believer to continually modify personality and behavior into Christ-likeness. Each believer bears a responsibility to not only allow, but to encourage new neurons (brain cells) and neural connections to further this transforming process. Yielding to the control and power of the Holy Spirit produces Christ-likeness. Indeed, we are urged in the Bible to have the mind of Christ or to think the same way Christ does (Philippians 2:5).

PAUL ALLOWING BRAIN PLASTICITY

The apostle Paul refused to have his mind, brain, and body (heart) distracted by anything from the past or present. He allowed the power of Christ's resurrection (Greek *symmorphizomenos*) to overcome any internal resistance to brain plasticity in conforming to Christ-likeness. He pursued Christ-likeness with the passion and persistence of a runner in the Greek games (Philippians 3:12–14, 21).

Brain- and mind-tuning in no way obviates the need for Bible study, prayer, praise, fellowship, and all the other facets of Christian living. The power to become like Christ doesn't come from pills alone; only the Holy Spirit gives spiritual life. However, the Bible asserts that our body is the "dwelling place, of God," and thus the brain-mind directs every spiritual fruit-bearing activity. Balancing brain chemistry for optimal functioning through the guidance of the Holy Spirit, significantly enhances your ability to "Love the Lord your God with all your heart, with all your soul and with your entire mind" (Matthew 22:37–38). At the same time, all the above biological, spiritual, and social processes are inseparably interwoven to protect believers from Satan's vicious attacks. We are called to destroy the works of the Devil. You are set free to flourish from within and without. The plan God has for you to fine-tune your total life will lead to your healing and a victorious Christian life.

OVERCOMING LIMITATIONS, REGAINING PLASTICITY

If you have inherited brain deficits or acquired neurochemical imbalance, due, for example, to environmental factors such as strong prescription medicines, poor diet, or substance abuse, the brain cannot participate efficiently in the work of transformation into Christ-likeness (Romans 12:2). If your neurons are oversensitive and have a tendency to release too much or too little of certain neurotransmitters[9] (messenger chemicals)—causing an imbalanced response—the brain cannot deliver, process, or store messages correctly about life in general or about the Holy Spirit.

Functional image studies and EEGs have demonstrated that head trauma, spontaneously occurring brain deficits, chemical imbalance, disease, or prolonged stress can cause entorhinal, hippocampal, or other cells to atrophy and eventually die, resulting in cognitive deficits. These centers of the brain are crucial for forming and making new memories and processing and retrieving old memories. Imaging studies have further demonstrated that other brain organs such as the amygdala, hypothalamus, and prefrontal cortex, which act as the executive branch of emotions, shrink in people with recurrent or chronic depression.

Prolonged periods of stress-related excessive cortisol release have been shown to deplete certain amino acids, enzymes, fatty acids, proteins, minerals, vitamins, hormones, or other brain

---

[9] Neuroscience mainly focuses on twelve major neurotransmitters, both excitatory and inhibitory: acetylcholine, dopamine, aspartate, epinephrine, norepinephrine, glutamate, phenylethlylamine and tyrosine. The inhibitory are gamma aminobutyric acid (GABA), glycine, serotonin and taurine—although over one hundred or so different neurotransmitters run through our bodies.

chemical messengers—resulting in breakdown of intercellular communication. These and other factors give rise to changes in the structure and function of the brain, causing disharmony and distortion which plunge many a helpless soul into spiritual misery and stasis. Something can and must be done to prevent such disastrous crippling. The brain's plasticity in the hands of a miracle-performing God defeats the Devil's claim on people and sets them free to worship God.

BRAIN PLASTICITY IS NOT A SECRET

God has not kept his desire for our spiritual expansion a secret because the filling of the Holy Spirit in a believer's life is limited only by the believer's degree of availability, flexibility, and mobility. Every biblical promise needed for spiritual expansion is freely available. For this supernatural living, God gives power to his children to manifest on earth the glorious reality that exists in heaven (Matthew. 6:9–10).

The teachings of the Lord Jesus definitively expunged man's disregard about God and His revelation. He said that all must respond to the revelation of love in Christ, which has made possible a full knowledge of God (Psalm 111:10; Romans 1:18–20; Colossians 2:3; Ephesians 3:17b–19).

Tuning your brain to promote Christ-likeness results in a Spirit-filled, joy-filled Christian life (Ephesians. 6:13; Galatians 5:22, 23; Ephesians 5:9; Colossians 1:10). If you recognize in yourself any manifestations of mind inflexibility, but have been unable to successfully change, allow the Holy Spirit to invade your mind, brain, and body. God is waiting for you to carry out His plans in your everyday life.

THE BELIEVER'S BRAIN IS FLEXIBLE TO CHANGE

When the various centers of our brains, especially those processing cognition, emotion, perception, memory, and conscience are not yet yielded to change by the Holy Spirit, the result can potentially execute depraved behavior. Our minds can be influenced by the world, flesh, or the Devil. Here is an example of a behavior that does not express heaven's reality of a flexible mind: ignoring and labeling members of the body of Christ by mere appearance or surface assessment. Jesus admonished Peter for being influenced by Satan's thinking (Matthew 16:33). Paul agonized over the Corinthian believers for not bringing every thought and lifestyle to the standard of Christ's lifestyle (1 Corinthians 3:3; cf. 2 Corinthians 10:5). The ultimate mark of Christ-likeness is unconditional love through the work of the Holy Spirit. Your mind being made flexible in the hands of the Holy Spirit enables you to accept a believer whom you would ordinarily ignore, as Christ has accepted you (Luke 6:36). That is just the beginning. Now we have the divine potential to give *agape* love—that is, sacrificial love—like that of Christ (1 John 3:11). Imagine being loved like that—by believers! Love is what makes life worth living. The Bible affirms that love lasts forever because God is love and God is eternal (1 Corinthians 13:8; 1 John 4:8). Such practical expression of Christian living is allowing God's will to be done here on earth as in heaven.

How can you allow your brain to be flexible in honoring God? Think of ways to honor God. Some examples follow:

- Meditate, pray, praise, and give thanks to the supreme-ly esteemed Lord.
- Give your anxiety, fear, and emotional pain to the Lord. You will be amazed by the never-ceasing, ever-amazing,

overflowing blessings of His presence in every aspect of your life.

- Be in hot pursuit to taste experientially the love of Christ, together with God's people in worship. Then you will be filled with everything God has for you.
- Stay away from "neurotoxic" relationships! Their non-Christ-like influences can weaken you and lead you astray. Let tough Christians deal with the manipulating selfish lifestyle of others. There is a biblical way to find love, stay in love, and grow in Christian relationships for a lifetime.
- Visualize yourself with the Lord Jesus on a beach, a beautiful mountain, or beside a lake. Reap from the full companionship of the Holy Spirit. Remember to enjoy good breathing. These practices can expand your mind, elevate your spirit and instill peace.
- Establish a few good relationships with people who love God wholeheartedly.
- Maintain purity of thought and action in all situations.
- Let go of bitterness, anger, and resentment, and refrain from gossip.
- Eat a balanced diet according to your body's needs. Avoid overeating; it's toxic to the body and accelerates aging.
- Drink plenty of pure water.
- Regularly do some form of exercise that works for you to keep you feeling fresh and alive.
- Avoid tobacco, drugs, excessive alcohol, harmful foods, and compulsive behaviors that inhibit brain plasticity.
- Think and speak joyful, uplifting, encouraging words. Smile often!
- Listen to sacred music that lifts you to heaven in your spirit.

Feel like you don't measure up? Don't worry. If you feel daunted by the idea of practicing all of the above in your life, take heart. This is a lifelong process. Take one step at a time. Maintain reasonable expectations about what you can accomplish. And remember, your Heavenly Father and his Beloved Son and the indwelling Holy Spirit are with you from start to finish.

Discussion Questions

1. Why is brain plasticity important for a Christian?

Answer:

2. How do you allow the lifestyle of Christ into your being to change you from one level to the next in the likeness of Christ?

Answer:

3. What is your part in practicing brain plasticity in the body of Christ?

Answer:

4. How is God asking you to be flexible in allowing the Holy Spirit to renew your mind to grow in Christ-likeness?

Answer: (Measure yourself against the standard of Christ's life.)

•   In reading God's Word
•   In thought

- In eating
- In watching TV or movies
- In using the computer
- In other activities

5. Do you plan to take advantage of your brain's plasticity for proper spiritual formation?

Answer:

6. Do you see how brain and mind abuse (for example: through the use of drugs and alcohol) can become tools in Satan's hand? If so, explain how? And how can you avoid such abuse?

Answer:

Chapter Seven

The Story of John: Fine-Tuning the Brain

Let me share with you the case of John, one of many real-life inspiring stories. This story illustrates how the imitation of Christ is inextricably bound to harmonious functioning of our brain and body.

At age eleven, John K.* accepted the Lord Jesus into his life. He attended a Bible-believing church with his family, participated in Sunday school, and grew up like any other Christian boy. Nevertheless, he lacked motivation, and often felt blue and discouraged.

His symptoms did not include memory disturbance, inattention, disorganized thinking, or incoherent speech, though some medical practitioners thought he suffered from attention deficit hyperactivity disorder. He was not diagnosed with any kind of behavioral disorder. He had no alcohol or drug problem during his high school years. None of his siblings, parents, or grandparents suffered from anxiety or depression severe

---

*Real name and certain details have been changed to protect the identity of the patient.

enough to require medication. His parents did not smoke. According to his mother, there had been no obstetric or neonatal complications.

John somehow managed to finish high school and went on to college. While in college, he smoked marijuana a few times with friends but didn't like it. His problems persisted. He felt frustrated, weighed down, and burdened most of the time, though not because he was unable to handle the college workload. Rather it was because, in his own words, "I think I was born with some brain problem. I really don't know what it is to have joy in the Lord or to feel love."

He was riddled with doubt about God, spiritual healing, and himself; his self-esteem was low and he felt unhappy most of the time. He socialized, but his relationships were not satisfying and usually ended in disappointment.

Later, when John was under my care, he told me, "On many occasions, I cried out to God to heal me. I often confessed my sins and asked the Lord Jesus to cleanse me with His blood and protect me."

He was anointed and prayed for repeatedly by spiritual leaders. Engaging in Christian and secular individual psychotherapy, group therapy, and seeing psychiatrists became a regular part of his life. No one could trace John's suffering to any traumatic event or situation that might have triggered his problem.

JOHN'S LIFE ON MEDICATIONS

By the age of 22, John's condition had deteriorated to the point that his thinking was greatly distorted and he was hearing voices. His psychiatrist prescribed various medications for anxiety, mood swings, depression, thoughts of suicide, hallucinations, delusional thinking, lack of motivation, and disturbed sleep. John had taken Ritalin, Lithium, Xanax, Elavil, Depakote, Zoloft, Corgard, Buspar, Prozac, Anafranil, Effexor and other drugs. He later confided to me, "I did not feel normal a single day when I was on all those drugs. Medication made me feel terribly sick, tired, agitated, and desperate. Sometimes I wanted to kill myself, but all I really desired was to be normal."

HE RECEIVED SHOCK TREATMENT

As a last resort, since medications, psychotherapy, and neurofeedback had not produced the desired results; John received electro-convulsive therapy (shock treatments) three times a week for two weeks. Subsequently, he suffered extensive memory loss; he was barely coherent, and his spiritual life was nonexistent. His parents said, "After the shock treatments, he was pacing back and forth in the psychiatric hospital like a zombie. He was constantly angry with us for giving him life; he cursed the day he was born." He had terrible mood swings. He turned his back on God and faith. He said it was not his choice; it just happened. Later John said of this sad time, "Something died inside me."

John's father continued, "Not long after this, his team of psychiatrists and other mental health professionals at the hospital determined they had done everything they could for John and discharged him to us, recommending the names of a few long-term mental health institutions."

John and others wondered if he were unable to release Satan's grip on his life because of some sin he or someone else had committed. Loving Christians reminded him that perhaps his suffering was God's design to strengthen and challenge him to overcome his difficulties and ultimately triumph in God's glory. His parents said that he was so psychotic that he couldn't sit quietly, pray, read the Bible, or go to church. He was truly a lost soul.

WAS GOD ORCHESTRATING A MIRACLE?

Little did anyone know that our sovereign God was orchestrating a miracle in John's life. At the appointed time, through God's providence, a physician suggested that our clinic might be able to help him.

At his first appointment, John asked in a sad voice, "Doc, do you know why I was born? I didn't ask to be born. Why is God torturing me like this? Why can't I be normal like everybody else and get a job, get married, and have a normal life?"

JOHN'S DIAGNOSIS, TREATMENT AND RECOVERY

Biochemical data, reflected the status of diagnostic studies from John's various physiological systems (immune, cardiovascular, pulmonary, gastrointestinal, genito-urinary, nervous, endocrine, skeletal, coetaneous, and hepatobillary). History obtained from family members, plus nutritional and spiritual insights, confirmed my initial impression that the source of John's pathology was biochemical imbalance in his brain, perhaps with cell damage in certain areas. He was deficient in more than the four primary neurotransmitters (acetylcholine, dopamine, GABA—Gamma Aminobutyric Acid—and serotonin) and had a suppressed hormone system.

All of this information, obtained with the cooperation of John's devoted parents, along with God's guidance, fostered a deeper understanding of John's problems and the development of a treatment plan. His brain chemistry imbalance affected every aspect of his life. His treatment plan included nutritional supplements, diet, and homeopathic remedies to repair his brain's irregularities and achieve optimum balance or homeostasis.

John and his parents were instructed in the importance of diet and nutrition to detoxify John's body and provide a solid foundation for re-establishing health. He was asked to eliminate all processed, sugar-laden foods and soft drinks. He received a variety of food-based nutritional supplements and homeopathic medicines to balance his brain functioning and support overall physical health.

QEEG[10] and ERP[11] were utilized to clinically assess changes in the electrical activity of John's cerebral cortex at various regions. The results were used to calculate numbers correlated with blood flow and energy consumption in various regions of his cortex. In the past, I have successfully treated hundreds of patients mostly without the use of QEEG and ERP methods. In John's case QEEG was primarily used for diagnostic purposes, hence these tools are not always essential in treating the milder cases. QEEG and ERP methods afforded a set of non-invasive tools to assess resting and evoked brain activities. Computer-assisted neuro-feedback and biofeedback may require as many as 30 to 50 or more sessions. In many instances the results can be excellent.

In short, after about a month of integrated treatment, John's QEEG map displayed a wholesome decrease of right side brain wave activity, and the left prefrontal cortex (frontal lobe) was firing at a rapid speed. This lobe plays a major role in performing many difficult and complex functions, including activities such as planning, feeling, thought, organization, critical thinking, control of emotions, judgment, joy, and happiness. This

---

[10] QEEG (quantitative electroencephalogram) measures the cerebral cortex activity, digitizes the analog signal by taking mathematical information from wave form, and saves the information on a hard disk. The computer then recreates the wave forms mathematically and displays them on the computer screen. Research has shown that QEEG permits a highly objective and reliable analysis of brain functioning.

[11] ERP (event-related potentials)

was indicative of a shift to a more balanced functioning in this part of his brain. His left side showed more activity, indicative of happiness, joy, or even mania in certain instances.

Three months later John was placed on an intensive training program. The training consisted of motivational techniques to focus and strengthen his desire for complete recovery, life management skills, Bible-based interpersonal therapy, and modification of habits and attitudes.[12]

He received Bible-based counseling that focused on identifying and correcting his false assumptions, unjustified generalizations, and distorted thinking. With good diet and nutritional support, appropriate supplements and homeopathic remedies, lots of *agape* (loving care), Bible studies, prayer, and fellowship, John obtained much relief from his imprisoning misery.

Within six months, about 70 to 80 percent of his symptoms were gone. He was trained to be aware of his specific physical and mental needs so that he could select appropriate supplements to maintain his improved status. He was assisted in the development of strategies and direction for managing his life better.

Although John's case was severe, and his problems have not been completely eradicated, he is better able to focus, maintain meaningful employment, and enjoy life. He often notes how far he has come through God's grace.

SADNESS REPLACED BY JOY AND POWER

Spiritually, John discovered an exciting new life and a new hunger for God and joy in the triune God—hunger and joy

---

[12] He had previously received 25 neuro-feedback treatment sessions for depression, on a neurosearch 24-channel unit (Lexicor Corporation). The changes following the neuro-feedback treatment occurred very slowly and were not always seen at the site of training.

that had eluded him for years. He behaved like a person who was newly introduced to life. With an almost childlike faith and sincerity, he tirelessly shares his testimony with people telling them how the Lord has healed him. He feels keen compassion for others' suffering. At last John is able to experience God's love; and he is able to cooperate with the Holy Spirit to pursue the spiritual work of transformation into Christ-likeness.

FOR REFLECTION

A number of factors may have influenced John's brain, resulting in severe malfunctioning. No doubt he had a constitutional predisposition to depression, exacerbated by poor diet and lifestyle. Considering his already compromised state, he may have been inordinately sensitive to the disorganizing effects of marijuana. His pathology was deepened by excessive dosing of many harsh medications over several years, distorting the structure and function of his brain.

Electroconvulsive therapy, a barbaric and desperate measure, did further damage to the integrity of his cerebral functioning. It is also possible that childhood immunizations may have contributed to his miseries.

DIAGNOSTIC DILEMMA AND MISUNDERSTANDING

Sorting out the many components of John's problems—brain dysfunction, neurochemical imbalances, lack of motivation, character traits, nutritional deficiencies, maladaptive habits and attitudes, negative life experiences, and spiritual stasis— posed a challenge for everyone involved. He had often been misunderstood; it's easy to attribute the lack of Christ-likeness in individuals to their negativity or carnality. In making this attribution, we hold such people morally and spiritually responsible for their own suffering. Such social bias and misunderstanding can only contribute to further dysfunction, feelings of rejection, and misery in a suffering individual's life.

THE EFFECTIVENESS OF AN INTEGRATED BIBLICAL APPROACH

The multidimensional course of treatment that enabled John to regain his health, emulate the Lord Jesus and receive God's blessings, consisted of natural gifts from God—herbs, amino acids, vitamins, minerals, wholesome foods, and homeopathic remedies prepared of simple substances from the earth. Added to that was the unwavering love of his parents and the brotherly love and dedication of the clinical team and of his spiritual counselors (Romans 15:13; 2 Corinthians 9:8; 2 Peter 1:5-8).

BITTERNESS AND PAIN WERE CONQUERED

Although he suffered great mental agony, John gradually improved, one behavior at a time. Bitterness and pain loosened their grip on him as he regained his health. His testimony of God's care, love, and power is poignant; Christ-like compassion and love flow from him to other suffering people. He realizes that our sovereign God in His infinite love and wisdom was working out all the details for the good of everyone.

Tuning the brain may be a battle against deeply engraved negative images. While the believer has a personal responsibility to cooperate with God, the Holy Spirit creates the desire for transformation, and He also gives us the ability to fulfill our responsibility by being empowered by Him (Philippians 2:13; 2 Corinthians 9:8; Ephesians 5:18).

Stories like John's serve as a reminder that what happens in the physical brain is crucial to the restoration of spiritual, mental, and emotional balance. Fixing the functional and structural irregularities of the brains of suffering believers can bring much joy and build strong character in them. In turn those restored individuals can bring much joy and love to themselves and to the members of the body of Christ! Imagine the privilege of comforting those in trouble (2 Corinthians 1:3-4).

Discussion Questions

1. Think of the great power of healing. Are there different kinds of healings? How do you see healing at work in your daily life?

Answer:

2. Do you believe that our transformation into Christ-likeness is tied to our relationships to other believers? (1 John 4:20)

Answer:

3. Have you seen some Christians receive physical and mental healing while others do not experience healing? Why do you think that is?

Answer:

4. Do you know a believer with a neurobiochemical imbalance who is driven to doubt God and walk away from faith? Why? How can you be of service to that believer?

Answer:

5. What are your thoughts about Christians needing to be more involved in helping people with severe brain deficits? "Spirituality that God our Father accepts as pure and impeccable is to take care of orphans and widows in their distress. And keep oneself from being corrupted by the world" (James 1:27).

Answer:

Chapter Eight

Identifying and Changing Unhealthy Nerve Cells, Inherited Disease Tendencies, and Brain Chemical Imbalances

How do we identify specific unhealthy nerve cells, constitutional disorders, or brain chemical imbalances? And how do we correct these problems? I have partially addressed all these and other related issues in earlier chapters. But in this chapter, we will further examine these questions.

DIAGNOSTIC IMAGING, NANO-CYBORG TECHNOLOGY, GENOMICS, AND SURGERY

At present, structural and functional neuroimaging by the use of computer tomography (CT), functional magnetic resonance imaging (fMRI), single-photon computed tomography (SPECT), pharmacological studies, cognitive tests, functional assessments, and genetic analysis have not entirely proven diagnostically reliable, clinically specific, or reproducible to accurately identify neurobiological deficits in adults or children.

Laboratory testing now permits measurement of a few neurotransmitters. But nano-cyborg technologies[13] pharmacogenomics[14] and related technologies are advancing rapidly, and new breakthroughs in those sciences can prove valuable in the near future to determine crucial brain functions and their dynamic balance.

Some neurosurgeons, scientists, psychologists, and psychiatrists are involved in treating neurological and psychiatric disorders by implanting electrodes in the brain or on the surface to beneficially alter its function. Another recent innovation, repetitive transcranial magnetic stimulation (rTMS), employs electromagnetic fields to alter brain activity, providing temporary relief of depression and other emotional conditions. There is also a new technique, vagus nerve stimulation (VNS), that works much like installing a cardiac pacemaker. The pacemaker (generator) is programmed to deliver a mild electrical impulse for about 30 seconds every five minutes, 24 hours a day. Psychosurgical procedures, however interesting, are invasive, expensive, and mechanistic. It is much better to prevent the need for such heroic measures by early discovery, by intervention, and by controlling the gene expression through gentle, natural remedies.

---

[13] ***Nanotechnology*** is the science of working at an atomic or molecular level using "nano" scale tools. A nanometer is one billionth of a meter in length. The width of the DNA molecule is 2.3 nanometers. In the future, for example, microscopic machines "nanobots," may help deliver neuro-regenerative nutrients to damaged brain cells. Nanotechnology combined with electro-microchips (cyborg technology) implanted in the brain, type thoughts on a computer screen in patients who are physically in a vegetative state.

[14] ***Pharmacogenomics.*** Genomics is the study involving the mapping of the functions and interactions in the pattern of our genes, called single nucleotide polymorphisms (SNPs). This research can be used to map genes to nutritional supplementation and medication designed to fit one's specific genetic pattern that regulates the brain and other functions This miniaturization of technologies will expand spiritual and other healing potentials.

CONTROLLING GENE EXPRESSION
AND IDENTIFYING ABNORMALITIES

Gene mapping has revolutionized our understanding of why some people get sick and others don't. An even more exciting reality is the fact that numerous genes associated with many disorders can be re-programmed with God-given natural remedies. That's how God wants us to treat our brain and bodies! On the earth and in the oceans, with the myriad mineral, botanical, and animal resources, God has provided abundantly the means to heal all the ailments that afflict the human frame. Yes, that is the God-designed way of life.

Our *genotype* is our inherent genetic blueprint that provides our bodies with a list of directions that can guide our body's function. But our *phenotype* is our present physical being. Our present lifestyle has considerable influence on how our genes express themselves. Imagine the genome as a bunch of firecrackers. The firecrackers are constructed in such a way that they cannot explode unless we ignite one or more of them. Because our bodies have certain genes that predispose us to disease, that doesn't mean we will get sick. We become sick when the gene is expressed (activated). But we can regulate the expression of our genes by wholesome eating and living and by optimizing our natural healing abilities, repairing cognitive deficits, and by utilizing any other natural interventions, many of which are mentioned throughout this book.

For example, through wholesome diet and natural remedies, we can turn off cancer-promoting genes, turn on anti-cancer genes, reduce inflammation, and strengthen the immune system. As indicated earlier, laboratory studies can provide some therapeutic guidance for restoring neurotransmitter and hormone balance. Lessons learned from experiments in mice brain cells and biochemical studies have identified abnormalities in nerve cells and the neurotransmitter system that are diagnostically and clinically useful. In addition, electroencephalography (EEG); quantitative electroencephalography (QEEG); brain electrical activity mapping (BEAM); written screening tests; neuropsychological, cognitive, blood, saliva, and urine tests corroborate findings of abnormal neurobiology. These diagnostic tools have been used by experienced practitioners to identify specific neurotransmitter imbalances or certain cortical abnormalities that facilitate identification and treatment of deeply embedded pathologies in the brain.

Further, clinical knowledge gained from numerous studies conducted worldwide and years of clinical practice by many doctors using diet, nutritional supplements, herbs, homeopathic remedies and vitamins have shown us how to safely use these substances to correct numerous faulty brain functions.

Despite the slow progress of determining crucial neurobiological deficits in the brain that affect health and spirituality, at present we have at our disposal sufficient knowledge, diagnostic acumen, and treatment strategies to effectively reverse or ameliorate many human afflictions that undermine our health and well being. Prospects for the addition of powerful new tools to our armamentarium are bright.

DON'T IGNORE SOME OF THE COMMON SYMPTOMS CAUSED BY VARIOUS FACTORS

- High levels of cortisol or other stress hormones such as norepinephrine and estrogen: in blood tests, people with depression show high levels of cortisol and other stress hormones. This can decrease spiritual vibrancy.
- Premenstrual Syndrome (PMS), pregnancy, postpartum depression, and hypothyroidism (underactive

thyroid gland) are common in women in the United States. Women are susceptible to interactions of high stress hormones and imbalances in female reproductive hormones, and their difficulties can be greatly exacerbated by use of oral contraceptives or HRT.

- Previous spiritual defeat: If you have one or more episodes of severe spiritual assault due to brain imbalance, you are likely to experience another one.
- Medications: Several drugs—including antihistamines, antispasmodic drugs, muscle relaxants and many others—can aggravate brain imbalance and cause spiritual problems, severe anxiety or depression. Women may have more side effects with several tranquilizers, flu medicine (especially amantadine), steroids, and certain chemotherapy drugs. It is probably safe to say that illicit drugs, many strong conventional drugs as well as alcohol are harsh to the user's brain.
- Elevated plasma homocysteine is an independent risk factor for coronary heart disease (CHD).
- Diabetes, obesity, and associated symptoms can affect spiritual vibrancy.
- Of course, traumatic brain injury can cause many physical and spiritual symptoms.

But despite all the brain abnormalities and physical ailments that often spawn or worsen them, if you have a longing to overcome all your problems, God can provide the means for relief.

HUNGERING FOR CHRIST-LIKENESS

Wouldn't you want above all else a Christian life full of the joy of the Lord? Wouldn't you like to experience God's power in your life, with a single-minded, holy passion for God, a burning love for Jesus Christ, avid hunger for the Holy

Spirit, Christ-like love and compassion for people, a servant's humility, balanced power in witnessing, superior mental focus, emotional resiliency, and supernatural peace and calmness—even under severe stressful circumstances, sternest trials, and intense persecution? This is our birthright; this is what God desires for each of us, and this is why He sent His Son to show us the path to spiritual fulfillment.

SATAN TAKES ADVANTAGE OF OUR WEAK THINKING

Let's be honest: although the deepest yearning of every Spirit-filled child of God is to stay alert to prevent wandering into sin (2 Corinthians 2:11; Matthew 26:41), many of us—even Spirit-filled, mature believers—sometimes lack sincere, pure *agape* love for God's children. We sometimes show hatred, arrogance, pride, jealousy, hostility, hot temper, and bitterness. We suffer anxiety, fears, depression, schizophrenia, dementia, or other human weaknesses. Why do believers also suffer a lack of self-control and extremely foolish passions? Why do they fall deeply in love with the world, affectionately employ worldly ways, and why do they play games with the Devil? Why do many believers remain comfortable at a particular spiritual plateau by choice? Can you really pinpoint the precise cause? (1 Corinthians 7:31; 2 Corinthians 11:2; James 4:7; Revelation 19:7).

Is it due to genes, environment, physical, or neurobiological malfunctioning? Or is it due to sin, not being filled with the Holy Spirit, lack of personal commitment to God, or lack of faith in God's Word and His power? Or is it because we cannot discern Satan's tricks? Or are even the most faithful among us, due to living in a less than perfect world, susceptible to aberrant cravings and behaviors, nutritional, neurochemical and hormonal imbalances, resulting in mental irregularities, dysfunctional behavior, and decreased spiritual vibrancy?

Identifying and Changing Unhealthy Nerve Cells, Inherited
Disease Tendencies, and Brain Chemical Imbalances

I propose that all of the above play a role, and although we will address various issues, we will primarily focus on neurobiological flaws and brain deficits that interfere with the process of attaining Christ-likeness.

Unquestionably, this world is not our home, and the reality of day-to-day living doesn't automatically lead to perfect joy and peace. Those can be attained only by determined and consistent effort which will ultimately be rewarded in our heavenly home. The Lord Jesus asserted, "In this world you will have trouble" (John 16:33). Various degrees of suffering, sorrow, emotional distress, mood fluctuations, and pain are part of life while we live in this physical body. It's certainly not sin to experience pain in life. But we are challenged to be of good cheer and rejoice always. Paul penned these inspiring words from a prison dungeon (Philippians 4:4; cf. 1 Thessalonians 5:16; Psalm 95:1).

How is it possible to experience a full, abundant, fruit-bearing life; to remain centered in God, even in painful or life-threatening circumstances; to be able to sing, praise, and give thanks to God, even when persecuted? Tuning the brain with the goal of becoming like Christ in suffering for Him, provides a wholesome and powerful tool to facilitate this spiritual state of transformation. To put it differently, the question really isn't "Will I suffer?" but "Will I be able to respond as did Christ and His faithful followers when suffering comes my way?" It's God's sovereign plan that believers suffer for Christ for the sake of righteousness (Philippians 3:10; cf. 1:29). Paul said, "We also rejoice in our suffering, because we know that suffering builds patience: patience produces character; and character gives us hope" (Romans 5:3–4).

The thought of future suffering doesn't have to induce fear, cause anxiety, result in catastrophic thinking, or suppress the ever-vibrating melody of the Holy Spirit in our daily lives. Jesus, knowing the secrets of human existence, said that we can't do anything about what may or may not happen tomorrow (Matthew 6:26–34). Remind yourself every day that whatever comes your way, God longs to make you like our wonderful Lord! So be encouraged, work hard, accept life's challenges cheerfully, and courageously, and be confident of His incomprehensibly boundless love for each one of us.

FOR REFLECTION

Body chemistry creates brain chemistry, and brain chemistry creates body chemistry; both influence the mind, and the mind influences both in a continuous feedback loop, these in turn influencing spirit, conscience, will, emotions, and soul. It's important to remember that the brain's plasticity enables it to continually change and modify personality. Each believer bears a responsibility to allow new neurons (brain cells) and neural connections to yield to the control and power of the Holy Spirit to produce Christ-likeness (Ephesians 4:23–24). No matter which variety of mental or spiritual deficit you have, you can find basic ways to improve your Christ-likeness.

The heroes of the Bible were invincible and powerful, but they weren't perfect. God turned their weaknesses into strengths (Hebrews 11:34c). God makes your total person strong (Hebrews 13:9c). How wonderful! God has a golden opportunity in store for you. In fact, even if you do not feel like a child of God due to your suffering, the reality of your being God's child does not depend upon your condition but completely on the gracious work of the Lord Jesus Christ.

The apostle Paul wrote, "You are the children that God clearly loves. So be just like Him, living a life of love, just as Christ did" (Ephesians 5:1& 2a). Paul wrote about placing our confidence in God, "In ourselves we are inadequate to claim any power to live the right way. It comes from God." Thus, Paul was able to say, "Practice all that you have learned, adopted, and seen from my examples," (Philippians 4:9a) because he followed the example of Christ.

Discussion Questions

1. What can you do in your life to further the spiritual reality of becoming more like Christ if you are called to suffer? Jesus said we are to be prepared for prosperity or persecution.

Answer:

2. Do you know that God has given you the power to change your brain and thinking to transform you into the likeness of the Lord Jesus? How is this achieved?

Answer:

3. Are you willing to trust other believers to help you when you need it?

Answer:

4. Can you write down a history of your participation in helping people of God in the past and now?

Answer:

Chapter Nine

Foods to Fine-Tune
Your Brain for Power

The simple fact is that the foods we eat have the power to prepare our brain and body to cooperate with the Holy Spirit in the process of fine-tuning us into Christ-likeness. On the other hand, we can hamper our ability to be transformed if we eat poorly. Poor diet generates much internal discord, which we experience as decreased ability to handle stress plus many other symptoms such as fatigue and irritability. Our body's impaired stress reaction can cause us greater stress, resulting in a snowball effect. Foods loaded with super-antioxidants, good protein, and complex carbohydrates can reduce brain fatigue and boost our energy. Plan carefully before you go shopping; buy foods that are both healthy and delicious. Eat well-balanced, nourishing, and varied meals. Avoid overeating and minimize refined carbohydrate foods, specifically white sugar, honey, dextrose, fructose, rice syrup, white flour products, etc. Limit unfermented soy products. They contain chemicals such as phytates and protease inhibitors that could cause more harm than good. Miso, tamari, soy yogurt, and shoyu are extraordinarily beneficial foods containing valuable enzymes, fortifying the blood, strengthening the body, and even conferring some protection against injury from ionizing radiation.

QUICK, SIMPLE, AND DELICIOUS FOOD PLAN

If you experience high levels of stress in your daily life and could use some extra energy and brain power, here are some sample recipes for an entire week to give you a practical start in promoting optimal spiritual health. Drink plenty of water or teas between meals throughout the day. Feel free to combine, mix, and alter these meals to suit your taste and particular needs. Use these suggestions to stimulate your creativity.

Monday

Breakfast: It is the most essential meal of the day, so do not skip it, especially on Sundays! Start every morning with 1 to 1½ cups warm or room temperature water, followed by breakfast 15 minutes later. Eat ½ cup granola, containing nuts, oats, barley oat bran, brown rice, millet, and dried or fresh fruits. To this add a half-ripe banana, peaches, an apple, or other fruit and add ½ cup nonfat yogurt, nonfat milk, or orange juice. If you have special nutritional needs, take your supplements. Some may like to eat one omega-3 egg with ¼ cup liquid egg white.

Midmorning snack: Herbal tea or diluted fruit juices; an apple, peach, or nectarine or ½ oz. low-fat cheese. Another combination would be popcorn or rice cakes with sesame tahini or almond butter.

Lunch: Eat a fresh garden salad containing lettuce, cabbage, carrots, beans, sprouts, tomatoes, and beets, etc. Use olive oil or low-fat or nonfat salad dressing. If you like turkey, add 1½ oz. turkey breast, chopped.

Afternoon snack: Carrots, apples or some other fruit.

Dinner: A cup of miso soup or steamed or boiled brown rice or whole-grain vegetable pasta (without eggs). One skinned and baked chicken breast mixed with ½ teaspoon of fresh chopped thyme, bay leaf, and peeled fresh ginger. Steamed broccoli or cauliflower, steamed kale, or other leafy greens enriched with a little olive oil, sea salt, and herbs of your choice.

Bedtime snack: One cup chamomile tea or warm milk.

Throughout the day: Drink filtered water between meals.

Tuesday

Breakfast: One or more eggs with cheese, sautéed finely chopped onions and broccoli with sea salt, pepper, basil, or other herbs.

Midmorning snack: Fresh apple and carrots or similar substitutes, or ½ oz. low-fat cheese and tea.

Lunch: ½ cup mixed berries or peaches. Multi-grain pita stuffed with mixed vegetables and cheese of your choice.

Afternoon snack: Fresh peach or nectarine or sliced pineapple.

Dinner: Asian combination (steamed or boiled brown rice, beans, cabbage, or sprouts, mildly seasoned with Japanese teriyaki or tamari sauce; add watercress, tomatoes, celery, and peppers as you like). One serving of fish or turkey breast seasoned with fresh onions, garlic, basil, and 1-inch of fresh peeled ginger; fresh fruit dessert, or fruit salad. Or try a serving of winter squash (acorn, kabocha, etc.), baked or steamed with tamari and sesame tahini.

Bedtime snack: ½ or one cup warm milk or a substitute.

Wednesday

Breakfast: ½ grapefruit or an orange. Multigrain or buckwheat pancakes or waffles with ¼ cup egg white; unsweetened fruit or apple butter or topping; one glass of milk.

Midmorning snack: Herbal tea and 6 oz. soy or other cultured yogurt.

Lunch: Chicken-lentil soup with ¼ cup chopped celery, ⅛ cup onion, ¼ cup diced red or yellow bell pepper. Mixed salad.

Afternoon snack: Any fruit or one puffed rice or graham cake and herbal tea. One or two slices of toasted spelt bread, with butter, cinnamon and xylitol (a sugar substitute).

Dinner: One cup of miso soup, ¼ skinned and baked chicken or meat loaf with ¼ cup of chopped onion, ½ cup mushrooms and ⅛ cup [cilantro], roasted peppers, onions, and spinach. Fresh salad of red leaf lettuce, endive, chicory, and diced parsley. Xylitol-sweetened chocolate pudding—½ cup.

Bedtime snack: One cup warm milk or chamomile or other nighttime tea. Add two or three rice cakes if you wish.

Thursday

Breakfast: One or more "omega-3" eggs, ½ cup liquid egg white scrambled; add 1 tablespoon yogurt after cooking.

Midmorning snack: Fresh apple or carrots. Herbal tea.

Lunch: Pita pocket (whole-grain) stuffed with cooked vegetables, garlic, stone-ground mustard, and a slice of cheese. Vegetable juice.

Afternoon snack: Fresh fruits, whole-grain crackers, or one cup of miso soup with seaweed.

Dinner: Fish, chicken, or turkey skinned and broiled or fried in thin olive oil with Italian spices. Fresh, diversified salad. Fresh fruit or a slice of natural carrot cake.

Friday

Breakfast: Hot whole-grain cereal with tahini, xylitol, and a little sea salt or two slices of French toast made with two eggs.

Midmorning snack: Herbal tea, an apple, or two rice cakes with humus.

Lunch: Multi-bean miso soup with a variety of vegetables, including ginger, garlic, onion, tomato, and spices. One cup of brown rice with chopped scallions, pumpkin, or sesame seeds.

Afternoon snack: Fresh apple or yogurt.

Dinner: A cup of miso soup; 4-oz. fish or meat grilled with onions and spices, including curry powder or turmeric powder; steamed, sautéed broccoli, and cauliflower with garlic, tamari, and cumin. Fresh mixed garden salad. Fresh fruit salad for dessert.

Bedtime snack: Warm milk or chamomile tea. Goat milk if you like it.

Saturday

Breakfast: Multigrain pancakes or Belgian waffles made with egg whites. Spray Pam in the cooking pan. Fruit juice.

Midmorning snack: Multi-grain puffed cake with tahini or almond butter.

Lunch: Kale soup (with onions, garlic, carrots, green pepper, ginger root, and cabbage). Fresh salad greens with dandelions and nonfat dressing. Pineapple for dessert.

Afternoon snack: Whole-grain blueberry muffin.

Dinner: A cup of miso soup; boiled brown rice or corn pasta with mixed vegetables; steamed collard greens with melted butter and a touch of sea salt and black pepper.

Bedtime snack: Warm milk or chamomile tea with a rice cake.

Sunday Is the Lord's Day

Sunday breakfast is important to boost your body's ability to absorb, give, and participate in everything God has planned for you. Many skip Sunday breakfast or eat a doughnut and drink coffee on the run. To continue living that way is to live with an imbalanced brain! It can prohibit you from accomplishing all that God has in store for you.

Breakfast: Make your own cereal for breakfast if you like.

1 cup puffed rice or millet or puffed barley or ¾ cup raw rolled quick oats

2 tbsp. wheat germ

1 tbsp. wheat bran

1 tbsp. chopped almonds

½ ripe banana, chopped (sprinkle on a bit of cinnamon powder) or ¼ cup raisins

Combine all in a bowl, pour on milk or almond milk.

Midmorning snack: One large apple. Ten or fifteen unsalted almonds and green tea.

Lunch: 1 cup of miso lentil soup—it can give you about 15g. of fiber.

Stir-fry mixed vegetables with one skinless chicken breast (add garlic, onions, ginger root, or other spices). At end of cooking, add olive oil and/or butter or shoyu.

1 cup boiled brown rice

Afternoon snack: Carrot sticks and one cup of yogurt flavored with vanilla extract and xylitol.

Dinner: Broiled salmon or mako shark in your favorite spicy sauce with garlic, ginger root, and chopped onions if you like. Diversified fresh garden salad. Steamed mixed veggies. Fruits and yogurt for dessert.

Bedtime snack: Chamomile, mint, or some tea that relaxes you; add a couple of rice cakes or a piece of whole-grain toast.

Congratulations! Have a week filled with God's choicest blessings! Try Mexican, Japanese, Indian, Chinese, Mediterranean, and other aromatic, delicious dishes. Have fun creating delicious and sustaining food for the spiritual pilgrimage.

Chapter Ten

Discovering What Your Brain
Needs to Achieve Christ-likeness

Your minds were made new and you were taught to
think and live a new life that is created to be truly good
and holy just as God is.

—Ephesians 4:23–24

As indicated in previous chapters, lack of single-minded
passion for Christ can have multiple causes. The good
news is that they can be approached with multiple solutions. If
you need spiritual transformation, God is committed to meeting your every need in Christ. Have you ever participated in a
Holy-Spirit-filled awesome worship service that was a little bit
of heaven on earth, and you just wanted it to continue forever?
Well, if it hasn't happened yet, you may experience the spiritual
mountaintop as your brain is fine-tuned. This is your heritage
as a child of God.

Experiencing the Resurrection Power of Christ

A group of Christian mental health professionals who are acquainted with the brain's capacity for change recognize that the possibilities for Christ-likeness are boundless in believers who are passionate about Christ. For neuroscientists, doctors, and researchers in this field, there is clear recognition of the plasticity or transformative capacity of the human brain.

If you are not often able to experience bountiful spiritual joy, the empowering surge of the Holy Spirit within you, you can refuel and replenish your depleted neurobiological and spiritual reserves to experience the resurrection Christ. You can never exhaust the fullness of our Lord Jesus Christ (John 1:16; 2 Corinthians 12:9; 2 Corinthians 9:8). To realize this inexhaustible blessing ever more fully, we must provide our bodies with the bounty of healthy eating, vitamins, minerals, amino acids, enzymes, plant substances, homeopathic medicine, regular exercise, essential oils, aromatherapy, biofeedback, massage therapy, acupuncture, stress management, counseling, relaxation, proper breathing, adequate sleep, and other tools and strategies God has made available to His children.

Self-Assessment Determining Your Proper Supplement and Nutritional Needs to Balance Your Brain

Before you get started on the road to tuning your brain, keep in mind that God works in many ways to remove mental roadblocks, to unleash His boundless power, to restore His image of holiness in His children. I am convinced that when you supply your body and brain the nutrients they need from a rich variety of foods and natural medicines—combined with the supernatural work of the triune God—you allow the Holy Spirit to transform your biological clay into the spiritual image of Jesus Christ. With this spiritual and neurobiological interdependence in mind, I would like you to take the following self-test after prayer and thanksgiving:

PRAYER

My most gracious, loving Heavenly Father, I bless you.

I praise and worship you with thanksgiving.

Forgive my sins; remove my guilt, and fill me with your Holy Spirit; I thank you for your comfort and guidance.

I know my help comes from you, Lord.

Empower me to make the right choices today to overcome and defeat the problems that have kept me prisoner.

Please turn my deficits into blessings (Ephesians 2:4).

Enlarge my vision.

Lord, I allow the Holy Spirit to replace all the old past sins, abusive, painful memories, addictions, and obsessive sinful thoughts from my brain to be replaced by your love, truth, and purity (Philippians 4:8).

May my life beam with radiant health and overflowing joy.

Please prosper everything I touch.

I know you have promised that "I can do all things with the help of Christ who gives me strength according to my need" (Philippians 4:13; cf. 2 Corinthians 12:9).

Prepare me to expect things bigger than my past and my present.

I believe your promise that no weapon meant to destroy me will succeed.

Open my eyes to see the glorious things and relationships you have promised for me in the body of Christ.

I lift your name above all names I plead the power of the blood of the Lord Jesus, the power of His name, and the authority of the Scriptures to protect, heal, and provide for me.
I love to have your goodness and mercy to overflow in and through me. I pray all of these in the most mighty and matchless name of my Lord Jesus Christ.
Amen!

Fine-Tuning the Brain and Christ-likeness Scale

Circle the numbers on the right side corresponding to the following statements that best describe you in the past three- to six-months or more. One is a lesser degree of agreement and four is a greater degree of agreement. The numbers on the left will guide you to the recommended supplements, referenced on the following pages. The numbers on the right indicate the relative degree of severity.

Lesser .... Greater

____16–I make discouraging interpretations of every event in my life.

0 1 2 3 4

____16–Most of the time I am not thrilled about spiritual things and often feel discouraged about my Christian life due to unstable moods.

0 1 2 3 4.

____32–I frequently find more pleasure in worldly activities than spiritual activities, although I want to change.

0 1 2 3 4.

____9–I tend to be anxious about involvement in spiritual activities.

0 1 2 3 4

___9, 40, 41–I feel stressed about going to church.

0 1 2 3 4

___1, 2, 12, 13–I have difficulty concentrating in church or elsewhere.

0 1 2 3 4

___7, 9–I'm often irritable in church.

0 1 2 3 4

___12, 13–I have difficulty absorbing new information.

0 1 2 3 4

___19, 21–I often become sleepy in church.

0 1 2 3 4

___9, 34–I suffer panic attacks or fears in church.

0 1 2 3 4

___44–My dizziness/vertigo keeps me from going to church.

0 1 2 3 4

___43–My Tourette's symptoms keep me from spiritual involvement.

0 1 2 3 4

___ 21–I am diagnosed with a hearing disorder. (Call for free booklet.)

0 1 2 3 4

___ 1, 2–I am diagnosed with Attention Deficit Hyperactivity Disorder (ADHD): Inattentive, Hyperactive-Impulsive or Combined type.

0 1 2 3 4

___9, 40–I don't like to be around people.

0 1 2 3 4

___9–I am generally a very anxious person.

0 1 2 3 4

___9, 16–I lack self-confidence.

0 1 2 3 4

___ 9, 34–I have fear of failing. (Call for a free booklet.)

0 1 2 3 4

___16, 29–I'm a complainer.

0 1 2 3 4

___2–I am hyperactive.

0 1 2 3 4

___9, 34–I experience fears, phobias and nervousness.

0 1 2 3 4

___12, 13–I suffer from brain fog or mental dullness.

0 1 2 3 4

___5–I suffer from chemical and food sensitivities.

0 1 2 3 4

___5–I suffer from seasonal allergies.

0 1 2 3 4

___1, 9, 27, 41–I am generally an underachiever.

0 1 2 3 4

___9, 12, 41–I have difficulty making decisions.

0 1 2 3 4

___16–I'm bored with life.

0 1 2 3 4

___9, 16–Most days I feel guilty.

0 1 2 3 4

___20–I suffer with fibromyalgia.

0 1 2 3 4

___ 21, 24–I suffer from recurrent infections.

0 1 2 3 4

___16 or 20–I don't have enough energy and vitality.

0 1 2 3 4

___9, 41, 42–My hands and feet often feel cold.

0 1 2 3 4

___6–I think I may have an early stage of Alzheimer's Disease.

0 1 2 3 4

___9, 16, 20, 26–I have difficulty waking in the morning.

0 1 2 3 4

____10–My arthritis prevents me from going to church.

0 1 2 3 4

____26–I have difficulty getting enough sleep due to insomnia.

0 1 2 3 4

____16–I am usually sad, withdrawn, negative, and pessimistic.

0 1 2 3 4

____11–I have symptoms suggestive of autism.

0 1 2 3 4

____7–I have lots of unresolved anger.

0 1 2 3 4

____2, 7–I am agitated, "hyper," and irritable.

0 1 2 3 4

____23, 35–I experience severe PMS.

0 1 2 3 4

____37–I suffer from seizures/epilepsy.

0 1 2 3 4

____7–I fight with my spouse or other family members frequently.

0 1 2 3 4

____32, 38–I am addicted to pornography.

0 1 2 3 4

____32, 38–I am addicted to sex.

0 1 2 3 4

____32–I have obsessive-compulsive tendencies.

0 1 2 3 4

____25–I experience symptoms of hypoglycemia (low blood sugar) such as weakness, irritability, light-headedness, anxiety, mental dullness, and headaches when hungry).

0 1 2 3 4

____25–I crave candy bars, sweets, high sugar cereals.

0 1 2 3 4

___17–I have diabetes.

0 1 2 3 4

___17, 25, 42–I am sleepy after meals or in late afternoons.

0 1 2 3 4

___28–I suffer from menopausal symptoms.

0 1 2 3 4

___16–I suffer from major depression.

0 1 2 3 4

___16–I suffer from depression as a reaction to events or lapses in my life.

0 1 2 3 4

___16–I suffer from dysthymia, i.e., mild depression, sadness, negative attitude, lack of joy of living.

0 1 2 3 4

___16–I am diagnosed with manic depression or bipolar disorder, or I experience significant mood swings.

0 1 2 3 4

___16–I frequently think about suicide or death.

0 1 2 3 4

___36–I suffer from schizophrenia.

0 1 2 3 4

___3, 4, 18, 39–I smoke, drink alcohol, or use other harmful substances.

0 1 2 3 4

___3–I consume more than three cups of coffee every day.

0 1 2 3 4

___41–I experience chronic stress.

0 1 2 3 4

___16–It has been a long time since I felt strong pleasure.

0 1 2 3 4

___31–I tend to fall asleep suddenly and/or I sleep so deeply that others find difficulty waking me up.

0 1 2 3 4

1. *ADD* (Attention Deficit Disorder)

It is the most commonly diagnosed childhood disorder. But ADD is still a center of controversy regarding the legitimacy of the mass scale diagnosis and treatment with strong drugs.[15] Individuals with Attention Deficit Disorder display the primary symptoms of: inattention, daydreaming, carelessness, distractibility, forgetfulness, procrastination, and lack of foresight.

RECOMMENDED SUPPLEMENTS

Brain Food for Children (**EPA/DHA**—smaller capsules available for children), *ADD Relief* (chewable tablets), *Brain Igniter,* (1 capsule once every 3 or 4 days for children (between 8 and 13), *Neuro Complex* (this formula contains phosphatidyl serine and acetylcholine*), Supreme Focus, Natural 5HTP* at bedtime, *Ester-C* (chewable lozenges)*, GTF Chromium or 3-Chromium + Cinnamon Complex* and *Children's Multiple Vitamin.* **For Adults**: *Brain Food, Brain Igniter, Neuro Balancer, Men's/Women's Ultimate Multiple Vitamin* and *Vitamin B-1.* Avoid all sweets, processed foods, and soft drinks, including those sweetened with aspartame. Biofeedback/neuro-feedback sessions accompanied by Bible-based, multi-image brain training facilitate restoration of normal functioning in some cases.

---

[15] An article published in the New York Magazine on October 4, 2004 pointed out that many teenagers and their parents are apt to seek prescription drugs for enhancing performance and to escape pressures of life. Teenagers may take Adderall for studying and snort Xanax to come down off Adderall and Ambien or Sonata for sleep. The line between medical and recreational use is increasingly blurred.

Biofeedback/neuro-feedback may take as many as 30 to 50 one-hour sessions, in many instances producing dramatic and lasting results when accompanied by recommended nutritional supplementation.

2. ***ADHD*** (Attention Deficit/Hyperactive Disorder) & Oppositional-Defiant Behavior

There are two groups of symptoms that define ADHD. One is related to inattention and the other to hyperactivity and impulsive behavior. Individuals with Attention Deficit Hyperactivity Disorder, predominantly Hyperactive-Impulsive Type *usually* display six or more symptoms of hyperactivity-impulsivity and less than six symptoms of inattention. They usually show some of the following symptoms: hyperactivity, restlessness, inappropriate running and climbing, excessive talking, a tendency to interrupt others, impatience, impulsivity, haste, and rapid movements. The stimulant drugs Dexedrine and Ritalin, and the first non-stimulant drug, Strattera, are still the standard treatments. They are toxic and are not curative. It appears that children with ADHD have at least one parent who meets the criteria for a diagnosis.

RECOMMENDED SUPPLEMENTS: *For **Children**: Neuro Relaxer, Brain Food (EPA/DHA capsules for children)), GTF Chromium or 3-Chromium + Cinnamon Complex, Taurine, Natural 5-HTP, Ester-C, Royal Jelly, ADHD Relief* (chewable tablets) *Men's/Women's Ultimate Multiple Vitamin, Manganese, Vitamin B-6, Neuro Complex,; For **Adults**: Brain Food, Neuro Complex, Neuro Relaxer, Neuro Balancer* (take one tablet with dinner for one week and observe your progress for a week or as needed), *Men's/Women's Multiple Vitamin, 5-HTP* and *L-Taurine.* Avoid copper, shellfish, and colas. Reduce all sweets and processed foods like white bread, toaster pastries, and doughnuts. Biofeedback/neuro-feedback sessions accompanied by Bible-based, multi-image brain training can facilitate improvement.

3. ADDICTION

God is at work in you as you struggle to overcome your addiction. He will restore you. Don't be too hard on yourself—it can discourage you. Satan will make you feel as if you are hopeless. Take heart that by God's promises He is transforming you. For supplements see sections on Alcoholism, Drug Addiction, Sexual Addiction, and Smoking Relief. Acupuncture, electrical Vega treatment based on acupuncture meridians, biofeedback, or neuro-feedback with behavior modification can reduce the urge for various addictive substances. Remember, your value or worth comes from God. This is what the Bible says about God's love: "I have loved you with an everlasting love. I have embraced you with an unfailing love."

4. ALCOHOLISM (Also see Drug Addiction)

Alcoholism affects more men than women. Studies reveal that children of alcoholic parents are more prone to abuse alcohol than children of nondrinkers. It is possible that some children are born with abnormal levels of various neurotransmitters or defective receptors in the nucleus accumbens, and other sites of the brain. Chronic stress or anxiety also can promote brain deficiencies. Consequently, many seem to engage in artificial pleasure-producing activities. Alcoholism can develop at any age. Alcoholics usually deny their problem. In severe alcoholism, detoxification may require medical supervision. Chronic drinkers undergo personality changes and suffer mental, physical, spiritual, and social ill effects. People who repeatedly abuse alcohol or drugs develop a deficiency of most of the brain chemicals, especially dopamine. Depression, suicide, violence, crime, and marital breakdown plague alcoholics.

God can deliver you from every addiction and abnormal pleasure-enhancing activity. In the concluding verse of the beautiful sixteenth Psalm, David so eloquently wrote about God's loving care, "You will show me the way of life; in your presence is fullness of joy. You have made available to me endless pleasures at your right hand" (Psalm 16:11).

Are you thinking about quitting? Don't procrastinate; be accountable and open. Be serious about quitting and start by changing your way of thinking and living. Stay focused on your goal of becoming like the Lord Jesus. Let the Holy Spirit control you and give you pleasure through spiritual means.

RECOMMENDED SUPPLEMENTS: *Liver Detoxifier and Regenerator, Neuro Complex, L-Glutamine, Brain Igniter, Royal Jelly, Brain Food, Alcohol Urge Relief* (chewable tablets), *GTF Chromium, Men's/Women's Ultimate Multiple Vitamin, Ph Balancer, Vitamin C, Vitamin K, Choline/Inosital, DMG, L-Carnosine, L-Methionine, Vitamin B-12, Vitamin B-1, Zinc, L-Carnitine Liquid* (1 tablespoon morning, noon, and night to relieve the urge). Take *Neuro Relaxer,* (1 or 2 capsule(s) a day between meals to reduce anxiety, cravings, and sleep disturbance), and *Natural 5 HTP* at bedtime. *Liver Detoxifier and Regenerator* is essential to protect and reverse the toxic effects of alcohol, or utilize Naltrexone (a drug that blocks the pleasure effects of alcohol). Avoid all animal fats and processed or fried foods and sweets. UCLA research unequivocally concludes that you are better off to abstain from alcohol. You should participate in a support group during your recovery process. Studies and clinical use have demonstrated that Kudzu root extract effectively reduces the craving for alcohol. Pure Kudzu root is available at www.natureshospital.com.

5. ALLERGIES

If you have respiratory allergies with stuffy and/or runny nose, use natural *Sinus Relief Nasal Spray.* Identify and eliminate possible foods that cause allergies, animal dander, and other environmental triggers that cause allergic reactions. If you are prone to anaphylaxis, ask your doctor to prescribe a home emergency kit such as Ana-kit or EpiPen.

RECOMMENDED SUPPLEMENTS: *Allergy Control, Super Enzymes Complex, Ester-C* and *Allergy Relief* (chewable tablets). Eat yogurt or take *Acidophilus Complex* as needed. Also eat pineapple.

6. ALZHEIMER'S DISEASE INSIDE THE BRAIN

The progressive degeneration of brain tissue is characterized by the gradual proliferation of clumps of tangled fibers and sticky neuritic plaques called beta amyloid. Scientists link the disease to a gene that codes for the synthesis of apolipoprotein E (APOE), a substance that helps deliver cholesterol and triglyceride fats throughout body cells. The risk for Alzheimer's is dramatically increased in those with the genetic variant known as APOE4.

In a study based on military medical records, researchers found that head injuries in youth greatly increased the risk of developing Alzheimer's later in life.

The disease develops in the interior part of the brain known as the entorhinal cortex and slowly spreads upward to the hippocampus, the part of the brain responsible for forming and retrieving various kinds of memories. Eventually the disease makes its way to the cortex. As the disease spreads to various regions of the brain, social abilities deteriorate, along with perception of space and time. Severe mood swings, outbursts of anger, aggressive behavior, disorientation, odd gait, or loss of coordination, and loss of bladder and/or bowel control may ensue as the disease progresses. Sufferers may also experience episodes of fearfulness, deep apathy, depression, or complete loss of reality and speech functions. The brain shrinks in size and weight as the disease eats away healthy cells. At this stage, memory of all kinds and capacity for abstract thought processes are lost. Personality and spirituality are also destroyed as the brain dies away. There is nothing we know today that will completely regenerate the brain to its original form once the disease has destroyed a substantial portion of the brain.

The progressive nature of Alzheimer's disease is classified into three stages.

Stage I is characterized by progressive forgetfulness, loss of short-term memory, increased anxiety and sometimes depression. At this stage spiritual aspiration is usually lost or reduced to mere ritualistic repetition. In **Stage II**, past memory may remain intact; immediate memory becomes elusive. The early signs of disorientation and confusion become a daily experience. Writing difficulties and other distortions of cognitive functions take the victim further into a shadowy world. Initially the person is usually helplessly aware of his deepening predicament. In most cases, toward the end of Stage II, mood and personality rapidly deteriorate. In **Stage III** most people lose cherished memories, the ability to recognize loved ones, and even themselves. Delusions, hallucinations, passivity, and violent episodes may follow. In addition, most become bedridden, needing full-time hospital or nursing home care. Some may lapse into an unconscious state before passing away.

INTERVENTION

The sooner natural interventions are implemented, the more promising the outcome.

For some, progress with supplements will take time, based on the extent of brain tissue loss.

People with early stage Alzheimer's may usually show rapid improvement with supplementation and wholesome diet within one year. Others may take anywhere from one year or more to show improvement. If the disease has progressed to many regions of the brain, regeneration will take longer, and full recovery is questionable. When one-fourth or more of the brain is destroyed, it's your decision to give or not to give supplements. No matter how advanced the disease, some of the ingredients in the recommended supplements are capable of enhancing activity and inhibiting the rapid destruction of brain cells. Published studies also indicate these ingredients may protect healthy people against various types of degeneration that occur in the aging brain. What's good for the brain is generally good for the heart.

Proven Tips:

1. Establish a consistent and familiar routine.
2. Four to six small meals are recommended.
3. Taking an afternoon nap is helpful for brain regeneration. You need at least eight hours of sleep in the night. If you cannot sleep well, take sleep supplements.
4. Rocking chairs seem to help reduce anxiety, frustration and depression. Rocking also increases motivation to walk.
5. Eating a balanced natural food diet (consisting primarily of whole grains, legumes, fresh vegetables and fruits, with or without a small quantity of animal products— preferably all organically raised) will slow mental deterioration, assist the process of cleansing the body, improve energy level and wellbeing, and substantially enhance the efficiency of nutritional supplementation.

Diet is a vital part of any treatment plan for Alzheimer's disease and related dementias. If chewing foods is difficult, purée them in a blender and concentrate on improving the quality of diet and assuring thorough chewing of foods, even those that are puréed.

6. Closely related to diet, the following also warrant consideration. Adequate intake of pure water, generally one to three quarts daily, is very important, especially during the first few months of dietary change or supplementation. These measures prompt a cleansing detoxification of the body. Avoid food or drink that has been heated, cooked, or stored in aluminum or fluorocarbon-coated (e.g., Teflon) cookware, since both aluminum and fluoride compounds are neurotoxins. Do not neglect God's most basic gifts: sunshine, a vital nutrient taken in through the skin and eyes (take off your glasses and expose your eyes to indirect sunlight with eyes open, direct sunlight with eyes closed); fresh air and contact with the earth—walk barefooted on grass, take walks in beautiful natural places, plant flowers if you can, enjoy the sunrise and sunset, those wonderful demonstrations of God's glory. Bathe or shower with filtered water to keep your body clean and fresh; vigorously rubbing the skin with a terry cloth towel is stimulating and beneficial.

7. Evidence based on observation suggests that Alzheimer's Disease may develop following emotional trauma (loss of a loved one, deep disappointment, major setbacks in life, etc.) or in those drifting into a state of emotional resignation. Attention to emotional issues and attitudes—plus creating an environment of pleasure, lively interest in life, joy, gratitude, friendship,

creativity, prayer, and spirituality—may be crucial to the long-term success of any regimen for the prevention or treatment of Alzheimer's and related degenerative disorders.

Suggestion for Support. Pray and act.

The responsibility of taking care of a person with Alzheimer's can be overwhelming. Bible-believing churches in nearby cities can get together, organize and provide safe, loving, friendly day care centers for our suffering senior saints. Meantime, look to adult day care centers, support groups for caregivers, medical, social, or family counseling groups.

RECOMMENDED SUPPLEMENTS: *Brain Igniter* and *Brain Food* (give both together), *Male Performance Support, Neuro Balancer* if depression is present, (take it alone with food, i.e., not with other supplements), *Neuro Complex, L-Carnosine, DMAE, Clarimen GC* (Creatine Monohydrate), *Men's/Women's Ultimate Multiple Vitamin, Natural 5-HTP* or *Melatonin* and *B6* at bedtime, *Advanced Gamma Vitamin E, Vitamin B-12* (only in the daytime), *Neuro Relaxer* (take only as prescribed on bottle), *L-Carnitine Liquid, Heart Prolongevity, Bone Density Calcium* (with magnesium and vitamin D) and *Coral Calcium Plus* (rotate monthly), *Vitamin K, Immune Enhancer I* and *II, Grape Seed/ Skin Extract, L-Taurine* and *Alzheimer's Relief* (chewable tablets). You may add additional CoQ10 (made in Japan). Volume 3 contains detailed information on Alzheimer's, other brain diseases and the use of DMAE, Pregnenolone, and growth hormone formulas. *Galantamine* is included in Neuro Relaxer, which is widely used for the prevention and treatment of Alzheimer's Disease. *We are in the process of finalizing a formula that contains the best of many supplements effective in the prevention and treatment of Alzheimer's Disease in one bottle.*

7. ANGER MANAGEMENT

(Explosive Temper, Mood Swings, Sudden Violence, Intermittent Poor Memory)

"A foolish person allows his anger to run wild, but a wise person keeps himself under control" (Proverbs 29:11).

Most events in our life evoke many emotions within us and we need them. We regulate them almost spontaneously based on our consciousness and other factors. An exaggerated response to our emotions can lead to undesirable consequences.

Regarding an angry temperament, we find the causes are many. These include perceived threat, jealousy, resentment, deprivation, various mental or physical disorders, a history of abuse or neglect in childhood, permissive or inconsistent upbringing, modeling of an angry parent, painful feelings or unresolved bitter conflicts, street drugs, toxic effects of certain medications, and synthetic food additives or alcohol. Often several of these factors combine to create the angry person.

Essentially, uncontrolled anger is a bad habit, so learn to control your emotions. Every habit—good or bad—has a corresponding neural pathway in the brain. Indulge a habit and an epinephrine rush releases a flood of angry hormones and neurotransmitters that in turn activate the amygdala and the prefrontal cortex that is responsible for reducing the inhibition capability of your brain. When you cool down, your brain can call on the rest of the brain regions to handle your anger at an adult-level cognitive control of emotions. Then you can positively redirect your energy to do something that pleases God.

The brain processes that control anger in children, adolescents, and adults with hormonal and neurological deficits may explain why these groups show slow integration of planned positive behaviors that are stored in specialized regions of the brain. The Scriptures do not define any age group as incapable of loving Jesus Christ. All are capable of fine-tuning their behavior based on the lifestyle of Jesus Christ.

So the crucial strategies in coping with the anger habit at any age are to:

a) obey the teachings of the Bible to make proper decisions; avoid risky, antisocial behavior and control impulses;

b) "transform or fine-tune your mind" through the work of the Holy Spirit; and

c) the use of recommended supplements for anger management can significantly shift the odds in favor of self-control.

"Get rid of all bitterness, rage, settled feelings of anger, harsh words, lying and hatred. Instead, be kind and tender to one another, forgiving each other, just as God forgave you because Christ has forgiven you" (Ephesians 4:31–32).

"Stop being angry!

"Turn away from rage!

"Do not lose your cool—it only leads to harm" (Psalm 37:8).

"Spirit-controlled people regulate their emotions; they earn respect by being gracious to others" (Proverbs 19:11).

"It is better to be patient than to fight; better to control your anger than conquer a city" (Proverbs 16:32).

"Love blossoms when a fault is forgiven, but those who talk about it separate friends" (Proverbs 17:9).

"Don't make friends or go around with hot-tempered people, or you will become like them and ruin your life" (Proverbs 22:24–25).

RECOMMENDED SUPPLEMENTS: *Anger Relief* (chewable tablets), *Neuro Relaxer,* (some would need extra GABA),

Vitamin B-6, 5-HTP, Brain Food, Bone Density Calcium with Magnesium & Vitamin D (calms the central nervous system) or *Coral Calcium* and *L-Carnosine.* Some may also need *Taurine, Glycine* and *Glutamine* to increase alpha brain waves and reduce the excitatory beta waves. Rule out allergic reaction to food and other toxic substances such as paints, alcohol, antibacterial sprays, etc. Biofeedback and neuro-feedback with transformation of brain image training can be quite effective. If no improvement in anger management is seen after 4–6 weeks, ask your doctor to do a laboratory test for (l.c.) Kryptopyrroles (the mauve factor 94). If anger is accompanied by depression, fatigue, dementia, or another disorder, look under those headings for recommendations.

8. ANOREXIA NERVOSA

Anorexia is a disorder characterized by a distorted body image and a phobia of becoming fat. This debilitating condition usually affects teenage girls or young women. It affects about one in 200 persons in the USA. It may begin with bulimia (bingeing and purging syndrome). Anorexia in most instances is a brain/mind disorder and may involve hereditary susceptibility. It's likely that the person with anorexia is depressed, conscientious, hypersensitive, shy, neat, compulsive, and given to unrealistic irrational guilt and striving for perfection.

RECOMMENDED SUPPLEMENTS: *Neuro Complex, Royal Jelly, GTF Chromium* or *3-Chromium + Cinnamon Complex, DMG, Neuro Balancer* (take 1 hour apart from other supplements), *Neuro Relaxer* (2 capsules with dinner), *Whey Protein, Women's Ultimate Multiple Vitamin, Anorexia Nervosa Relief* (chewable tablets), *Potassium, Immune Enhancer I* and *II.* Some anorectics may need *Zinc, Vitamin K,* and *Advanced Gamma Vitamin E.* If suffering from swollen joints, brittle nails, dry skin, constipation, and insomnia, see recommendations for those symptoms. If the heart rate, blood pressure, and body temperature are low, she or he must be given immediate medical attention. Eat five small meals high in protein. Avoid alcohol, caffeine, and sugar. (See also Bulimia.)

9. *ANXIETY* (See Also Social Phobia and Panic Attacks)

Anxiety does not indicate lack of faith, hope, love, or lack of the Holy Spirit's work. Anxiety is complex and part of our fallen emotions. You are not alone in battling anxiety disorders. Anxiety disorders are the second most common mental health problem in the United States, second only to substance abuse. National Institute of Mental Health (NIMH) statistics reveal that about 19 million Americans suffer from anxiety disorders.

Symptoms:

If your symptoms persist for six months or more, you are experiencing an anxiety disorder. Do you experience muscle tension, stress, irritability, fear, excessive worry, insomnia, excessive sweating, heart palpitation, blushing, nausea, obsessing over the "what ifs" of most things in life, a shaky voice, hot flashes, headaches, and other aches and pains without any apparent cause? If so, then you may be experiencing what is called Generalized Anxiety Disorder. Many different anxiety disorders are identified as: phobias, panic disorder, obsessive-compulsive disorder, Post Traumatic Stress Disorder (PTSD), social anxiety, generalized free-floating anxiety, or performance anxiety.

Social Anxiety:

People with social anxiety may be reluctant to use a public restroom or eat in a restaurant; they may even drop out of school or work due to various fears. In children and adults, social anxiety resembles the avoidant personality disorder characterized by self-consciousness and timidity. They may have poor self-esteem and consider themselves unattractive or worthless. They may experience panic or freeze in church gatherings. Panic and social anxiety often are accompanied by physical symptoms such as a racing heart, muscle tension, dry mouth, a shaky voice, nausea, blushing, sweating, and difficulty breathing.

An appropriate degree of anxiety or fear about real danger is normal and even healthy because it protects us from harm; but when it becomes excessive and persistent, it makes life miserable.

Performance anxiety is a subtype of generalized social anxiety in which symptoms are provoked by anticipation of performing in public and often persist even during performance.

Your Brain and Anxiety:

Different areas of the brain and diverse neurotransmitters may be involved in different anxiety experiences. If you suffer from anxiety, you need to understand that your thinking needs to change. "Anxiety" derives from a Greek word meaning "to have a split mind." For many people, changing thinking and vanquishing anxiety is greatly facilitated by taking appropriate supplements to balance brain chemistry. Treating your brain can help replace your needless anxiety with a mind set on heavenly things and thoughts that are "excellent and praiseworthy" (Read Psalm 103: 2–4; Matthew 6:26–34; Philippians 4:6–7 and Colossians 3:5). Stay close to God and His children! He knows what's around the next corner. Studies reveal that fifty percent of what we worry about never happens. Thirty percent focuses on circumstances beyond our control. Most of our anxieties and worries are needless. Give your concerns to God because He has promised to give us peace and protect our minds, brains and bodies in Christ Jesus. Anxiety may spur us on to think things through, put problems into perspective, and find comfort in faith and realization of God's love. I have seen many of our Christian patients recover fully from their anxiety and panic disorders when the brain is balanced with supplements, bio-or neuro-feedback and balanced biblical thinking. The Bible says, "But the Lord is faithful; He will give you strength and protect you from the evil one" (2 Thessalonians 3:3).

RECOMMENDED SUPPLEMENTS: *Neuro Complex, Royal Jelly, Brain Food, Anxiety & Stress Relief* (chewable tablets), *GTF Chromium* or *3-Chromium + Cinnamon Complex, Vitamin B-6, Neuro Balancer, Men's/Women's Ultimate Multiple Vitamin, Clarimen GC* (Creatine Monohydrate), *Vitamin B-12, Neuro Relaxer, L-Carnosine, Natural Sleep, 5HTP* at bedtime (if unable to sleep), and *DMG.* You may need *Bone Density Calcium* (with magnesium and vitamin D) to raise your pyruvate level in the blood and brain. Take two Bone Density Calcium tablets 30 minutes before bed or *Pure Coral Calcium.* If you have experienced an adverse reaction to serotonin drugs like Zoloft, Paxil, and Prozac (SSRI'S), avoid methionine and copper. Also avoid coffee, caffeinated soft drinks, and ephedra-containing supplements or over-the-counter medications containing stimulants. Take 500–1000mg of timed-release *Ester C* or *other Vitamin C.* Also, practice stress and anxiety management techniques that can change anxiety-inducing thoughts and symptoms. Deep breathing, exercise, quiet biblical meditation, trust in God, and consoling contact with loved ones and fellow pilgrims can help to reduce anxiety and worries. Reducing some of your responsibilities may help. Listen to what Jesus says. Why are you distressed about tomorrow? Don't worry about tomorrow because each day has enough trouble of its own. Your Heavenly Father knows all your needs (Matthew 6:34a; 30c; 31a; 34b; 32b).

10. ARTHRITIS

As we age or due to diseases, structural changes occur in our joints leading to pain, loss of mobility, joint stiffening, swelling, muscle pain, and bursitis. Arthritis is not a single disease, but a general name given for many inflammatory diseases that affect all the joints, including our spine, hips and knees.

RECOMMENDED SUPPLEMENTS: *Natural Joint Integrity* is perhaps the best and safest supplement available in America for joint problems. *Natural Joint Integrity's* unique combination of 25 ingredients have been shown in a clinical trial to nutritionally support healthy ligaments, tendons, bones, synovial fluid, cartilage structure and joint mobility. Regular use of *Natural Joint Integrity* can rebuild new cartilage, reduce pain and inflammation, and in some cases prevent or reduce deformity. *Joint Pain Relief Cream* can give you pain relief. Also take a multivitamin and drink plenty of pure water. Early intervention by taking recommended supplements can help control the damage. Adequate intake of Vitamin D, K 1 & 2 and *Brain Food* (pure Omega 3) which can reduce serious joint damage should be taken daily and *Royal Jelly.* Avoid all refined or concentrated sugars; instead use xylitol, a natural sweetener. Eat avocados, fish, fermented soy foods such as tofu and tempeh frequently. Avoid the nightshade plants (tomatoes, potatoes, and egg-plant) which contain toxic alkaloids which deposit in joints and increase arthritic symptoms. Exercise regularly, such as moderate walking, swimming etc. Regular exposure to direct sunshine, facing the sun with eyes closed and no eyeglasses for at least ten minutes daily—may ameliorate arthritic symptoms by stimulating the pineal gland, a tiny organ deep in the center of the brain which is the master regulator of the endocrine system. Keeping your weight at the right level can help.

11. ASPERGER'S and AUTISM

Asperger's Syndrome is part of what is now called the autistic spectrum. The line between autism and Asperger's disorder is not always clear. Asperger's and autism should not be confused with ADHD. Many autistic youngsters are bright and talented; others are angry, agitated, and deeply disturbed; some suffer severe mental deficits, usually have perseverating thoughts and behaviors, and are often clumsy. Despite normal or superior intelligence, people with Asperger's have difficulty comprehending social cues and are unable to take hints, understand humor, or keep secrets. These children can take a severe toll on their families. The recommended supplement program is essential to enhance brain development and emotional balance.

The following general criteria for this condition are:

1. Social interaction impairment such as:
   a. lack of nonverbal communication, e.g., appropriate body language and eye contact;
   b. inability to socialize and develop age-appropriate friendships; and
   c. a tendency to isolate and a lack of interest in sharing with others;
2. Communication impairment such as:
   a. delay in speech development or absence of spoken language,
   b. inability to maintain conversation,
   c. repetition of words or phrases,
   d. lack of spontaneous make-believe play;
3. Repetitive behavior, activities and interests such as:
   a. fixation on a single interest,
   b. ritualistic behaviors or rigid habit patterns,

    c. repetition of body movements (e.g., clapping hands) or

    d. preoccupation with objects.

RECOMMENDED SUPPLEMENTS: *Brain Food, L-Carnosine, Neuro Balancer, 5-HTP* at bedtime, *Neuro Relaxer, Clarimen GC* (Creatine Monohydrate), *Children's/Men's/Women's Ultimate Multiple Vitamin* and *Autism Relief* (chewable tablets). Some would need additional specific RNA supplements. Some may need additional *Vitamin B6* [16], *Taurine,* and *Magnesium Citrate* to prevent loss of dopamine from the brain. Sessions involving computer-assisted neuro-feedback, and Christ-like character/brain image transformation sessions can do wonders in treating autism. See detailed instructions on the Web site. Moderate and severe cases should be treated under the supervision of an experienced health care professional.

12. BRAIN, MIND, MEMORY

Stretching the mental muscles by playing chess, solving crossword puzzles, and other mental challenges can prompt the growth of nerve cells only if your brain has enough brain nutrients. You cannot teach new tricks to a starved brain. Diet and lifestyle have a profound influence on mental health, supplying the brain with appropriate nutrients that prevent rapid death of brain cells and nurture growth of new, healthier cells. This can augment the benefits of wholesome diet and lifestyle.

---

[16] Excessive doses of vitamin B-12 can cause depletion of brain dopamine and serotonin, as well as elevated levels of lactic acid in the brain, all of which can result in increased anxiety. Therefore, if one is taking the multivitamin, additional B-Complex is not indicated. Since vitamin B-6 has an inhibitory influence on brain neurotransmitters, generous use of supplemental B-6 decreases anxiety, or you may get chewable ***Anxiety and Stress Relief*** tablets. For more information go to ***www.natureshospital.com*** or write to: Nature's Hospital, P.O. Box 217, Glendora, NJ 08029

RECOMMENDED SUPPLEMENTS: *Brain Food, Royal Jelly, Neuro Complex, EDTA* oral capsules (if you have a high level of LDL), *Brain Fog Relief* (chewable tablet), *Neuro Relaxer, Clarimen GC* (Creatine Monohydrate), *5-HTP* at bedtime, *DMAE, Neuro Balancer* (if depression or anxiety is present) and *Heart Prolongevity.* After 1 month, take *Immune Enhancer I & II, Vitamin B-1* and *3 Chromium + Cinnamon Complex* to prevent hardening of the arteries that supply blood to the brain. *See also Brain Fog.*

13. BRAIN FOG

Mental Fogginess can be caused by many abnormalities in the brain and body. Evidence suggests a neurobiological imbalance or slower brain metabolism; that is, a lack of strong stimulation of cortical brain cells on demand by reticular activating impulses can cause a lack of focus. Contributing factors are many, including poor diet, lack of exercise, ennui or frank depression, anxiety, chronic stress, and many constitutional conditions such as fibromyalgia and Chronic Fatigue Syndrome. These factors must be addressed. While you are cleaning up your diet, exercising, injecting wholesome and pleasurable activities into your life, and grappling with other factors as needed, appropriate supplementation can jump-start the brain and hasten the transition to a higher level of functioning.

Scientific research has shown that prolonged stress depletes hormonal, organ and body reserves while producing high levels of cortisol. Functional imaging studies and brain electrical activity measurements demonstrated that the amygdala, prefrontal cortex and other areas of the brain shrink in people with chronic stress, depression, or other chronic mental disorders.

Supplementation can enhance mental clarity, alertness, concentration, and memory. It can also increase cerebral energy level, promote smooth flow of electrical signals, and protect the brain from the injurious effects of stress, anxiety, toxins, and fatigue.

Suboptimal nutrition robs your body of good health! To ensure optimal health to cerebrovascular and cardiovascular blood supply throughout the brain and body, and to clear up your brain fog, add the following supplements.

RECOMMENDED SUPPLEMENTS: *Brain Igniter, Brain Food, Royal Jelly, Heart Prolongevity, Neuro Complex, EDTA* oral capsules (if there is reason to suspect that atherosclerosis is limiting blood supply to the brain or heart), *DMG, Men's/Women's Ultimate Multiple Vitamin, Clarimen GC* (Creatine Monohydrate), *Advanced Gamma Vitamin E, L-Glutamine, Vitamin B Complex-50* (1 capsule every 3 days, if taking a multiple vitamin), *L-Carnosine, Supreme Focus, 3-Chromium + Cinnamon, Grape Seed/ Skin Extract, Brain Fog Relief* (chewable tablets). These supplements can be purchased from *Nature's Hospital.*

14. BULIMIA

Those with this disorder consume large amounts of food and then rid their bodies of the excess calories by self-induced vomiting, enemas, laxatives, diuretics, or obsessive exercising. Because these individuals "binge and purge" and are able to maintain normal body weight, they often successfully hide their problem from others for years. The frequency of bingeing and purging can range from once or twice a week to several times a day. The reason for this behavior is an abnormal fear of becoming fat and an obsession with eating.

Bulimia typically begins during adolescence and occurs most often in women between ages 15 and 30; the condition is also found in some men. Many individuals do not seek help until their late 20s, 30s, or 40s. By this time their eating behavior is deeply programmed into their brains and bodies, making it more difficult to change. Continuing this destructive pattern for a prolonged period can result in dangerous nutritional deficiencies and metabolic imbalances. If you think you have reached a chronic state of bulimia, seek professional help at once.

Other symptoms include: cramping, dizziness, emaciation, low blood pressure, irregular heartbeat, broken blood vessels on the face, damage to the enamel of the teeth, irregular menstrual periods, swollen neck, and depression, sometimes with suicidal ideation.

RECOMMENDED SUPPLEMENTS: *Bulimia Relief* (chewable tablets), *Taurine, Neuro Complex, GTF Chromium, Royal Jelly, Whey Protein Powder, Neuro Relaxer, Men's/Women's Ultimate Multiple Vitamin, Magnesium Citrate,* or *Bone Density Calcium* (with magnesium and vitamin D). If you are taking the above supplements, you need not add extra *Zinc*. *5-HTP* is included in the *Neuro Relaxer*, but some may need additional *5-HTP* at bedtime to promote sleep. Christ-like character brain image transformation sessions, accomplished through computer-assisted brain wave measuring instruments, can produce amazing results. See also Anorexia Nervosa.

15. DEMENTIAS—VASCULAR, LEWY BODY, AND OTHER TYPES

Vascular Dementia (VaD) is the result of single or multiple strokes in the brain caused by loss of blood flow. VaD usually has an immediate, sudden onset following a stroke. Progression of VaD may manifest as deterioration in functioning, stabilizing for a time and then deteriorating again. Some examples of affected areas of the brain are vision, memory, and language. Some VaD risk factors are age (over 65), high blood pressure, heart disease, diabetes, poor diet, and a sedentary lifestyle.

Lewy body-dementia (LBD) is characterized by dramatic fluctuations in daily cognitive functions, visual hallucinations, delusions, paranoia, motor disturbances, and impaired balance and muscle rigidity. LBD is an aggressive disease that is relentless in destroying the brain, generally within five to seven years, much faster than Alzheimer's disease. Treatment is difficult, but diagnosis may not be difficult due to the presence of a gelatinous proteinaceous substance (Lewy bodies) embedded in the interior of brain cells, which can be identified by various means.

There are other types of dementia that do not clearly fall into one of the above classifications. The supplements recommended below are also appropriate for these other types of dementia.

RECOMMENDED SUPPLEMENTS: *Brain Food, Royal Jelly, Brain Igniter, Grape Seed/ Skin Extract, EDTA oral chelation* (if you have clogged arteries), *Neuro Balancer, Men's/Women's Ultimate Multiple Vitamin, L-Carnosine, Neuro Complex, Heart Prolongevity, L-Glutamine, DMG* and *DMAE*. After one month, take *Immune Enhancer I & II*. (We are close to completing research in formulating a supplement specifically for these dementias.)

About Galantamine: In a study in which half a dozen American medical institutions collaborated, galantamine (one of the ingredients in Neuro Balancer) was given orally twice daily, in doses of 8mg a day for the first four weeks, then 16mg a day for the next four weeks, then 24mg a day for the duration of the non-placebo-controlled study. This regimen produced remarkable improvement in memory, attention, visual-spatial tasks, reduction in apathy, depression, and hallucinations—and participants were able to perform routine daily tasks with greater ease.[17]

---

[17] Edwards, K.R., Hershey L., Bednarczyk, E.M., Lichter, D., Farlow, M., and Johnson, S. "Efficacy and safety of Galantamine in patients with dementia with Lewy bodies: a 12-week interim analysis." *Dement Geriatr cogn Discnd* (2004): 17: (Supp 1): 40-8.

16. DEPRESSION

Depression can deeply affect the way you feel about yourself and others, God, your environment, and everything in life. Depression appears to be the most common brain dysfunction, afflicting a large percentage of people. Depression can strike people of all ages and can go unrecognized for years. If depression persists more than a few months, it can significantly impair immune function, which can result in various types of pain, as well as increased susceptibility to infection. The subtle interrelation of high levels of stress hormones that are present in all forms of depression, immune function, and disease processes is an intricate web involving many factors such as diet, exercise, social interactions, spiritual development, and personal susceptibilities.

A growing body of mental health professionals sees anxiety and depression as symptoms of a single underlying condition. The American Psychiatric Association (APA) is referring to it as mixed anxiety depressive disorder.

Symptoms that may manifest in all types of depression:

- Sadness, melancholia, weeping, despair, feeling forlorn
- Suicidal thoughts, suicide attempts
- Anhedonia (joylessness, indifference to formerly pleasurable interests and activities), loss of motivation
- Lack of spiritual desire
- Feelings of inadequacy, loss of self-confidence
- Social withdrawal
- Difficulty concentrating
- Difficulty making decisions
- Mental dullness, brain fog
- Low self-esteem or feelings of worthlessness
- Hypervigilance and hyperscanning
- Fatigue or loss of energy

- Paralysis of the will, loss of self-control
- Restlessness
- Irritability
- Anxiety, agitation
- Frustration, angry outbursts
- Mood swings
- Sleep disturbance—insomnia or hypersomnia; sometimes with reversal of the sleep/wake cycle
- Lowered energy, listlessness
- Decreased appetite or overeating, indigestion
- Headache
- Back pain
- Lowered immune function, increased susceptibility

Causes of Depression

There is no single cause of depression. Many recent studies trace the causes of depression to nutritional deficiencies in the brain's glial cells and other abnormalities in brain chemistry or structure. Thanks to recent advances in brain research, neuroimaging, and neurochemical tests, doctors now know that many types of debilitating depression are imbalances in brain chemicals. This discovery makes it easier to diagnose and treat various depressions. Severe prolonged stress can result in depression by upsetting the balance of neurotransmitters in the brain. Depression often runs in families, arising from genetic predisposition and/or neurotic character structure. Food allergies, hormone imbalance, the weakening and demoralizing effects of chronic illness, malnutrition due to poor diet, and insufficient exposure to sunlight can result in emotional and mental imbalances, creating depression.

Reactive Depression arises as a result of emotional trauma—loss of a loved one, tragedy, financial loss, sudden disability, or other painful disruptive life events. It is usually a mild-to-moderate form that resolves with the passage of time. Unshakable faith in God and family and social contacts are important factors in mitigating reactive depression.

RECOMMENDED SUPPLEMENTS: *Brain Food, Royal Jelly, Neuro Complex, Grape Seed/ Skin Extract, Neuro Balancer, Reactive Depression Relief* (chewable tablets), *Men's/Women's Ultimate Multiple Vitamin, GTF Chromium* or *3-Chromium + Cinnamon Complex, L-Carnosine,* and *5-HTP* or *Neuro Relaxer* at bedtime to promote restful sleep. Linden leaf tea may also be helpful.

According to the American Psychiatric Association, there are three types of depression and mood disorders:

1. Dysthymic Disorder and its bipolar variant, Cyclothymic Disorder;
2. Major Depression; and
3. Manic Depression or Bipolar Disorder.

1. *Dysthymic Disorder* has less serious symptoms, but is chronic in nature. It can be considered a low-grade, more persistent version of major depression. The Greek word, dysthymia, means "bad state of mind" or "ill humor."

Cyclothymic Disorder literally means "circular spirit" and is often referred to as *soft bipolar disorder.* This affliction can be considered a mild, non-psychotic version of manic depression, with periods of relatively normal functioning or hypomania (elevated activity level) alternating with periods of mild to moderate depression. Recent research indicates that this common chronic type of low-grade depression often results from low self-esteem and negative thinking habits associated with lowered levels of activity of certain neurotransmitters, which may arise from an inherited predisposition or from negative, destructive environmental influences during the formative years. It is estimated that half of dysthymic people eventually experience an episode of major depression.

RECOMMENDED SUPPLEMENTS: *Neuro Complex, Royal Jelly, Brain Food, Brain Igniter, L-Carnosine, Grape Seed/ Skin Extract, Dysthymia Relief* (chewable tablets), and *Men's/ Women's Multiple Vitamin and GTF Chromium or 3-Chromium + Cinnamon Complex and Green Barley.*

---

2. *Major Depression* is one of the most serious types, characterized by overwhelming and sustained bleakness, often disabling, sometimes with psychotic or borderline psychotic loss of contact with reality. *Children and adolescents manifest many of the same symptoms.* Although the prefrontal cortex of the brain may be the primary site of malfunction in major depression, the whole brain is disordered to some degree.

The constellation of symptoms often found in children and adolescents with major depression are:

- Persistent sadness, pessimism, helplessness, hopelessness, guilt, despair, low self-esteem
- Insomnia or oversleep
- Mood swings
- Chronic indecisiveness
- Anxiety, irritability, agitation
- Inability to concentrate, make decisions, brain fog
- Fatigue, slow speech, slow movements
- Appetite loss or gain
- Weight gain or loss
- Crying fits for no obvious reason
- Suicidal thoughts, suicide attempts

RECOMMENDED SUPPLEMENTS: *Major Depression Relief* (chewable tablets), *Brain Food, Neuro Complex, Royal*

Jelly, L-Taurine, Bone Density Calcium (with magnesium and vitamin D), or *3-Chromium + Cinnamon Complex, Grape Seed/ Skin Extract, Choline/Inositol, Vitamin B-6, Men's/Women's Ultimate Multiple Vitamin, 5-HTP* or *Neuro Relaxer* at bedtime, *Green Barley, Neuro Balancer*—take *Neuro Balancer* with food, one hour apart from other supplements—*Brain Igniter* (if needed for mental clarity), *DMG,* and *Vitamin B Complex-50* (if needed).

---

3. *Bipolar Disorder or Manic Depression* Manic depression is characterized by cyclical mood swings between elation and despair. It is a variant of major depression and most often has a large inherited (genetic) component. It is a serious illness, usually arising from an inherited predisposition. It is often difficult to treat; it may require years to cure. In addition to the recommended supplements, wholesome diet, plenty of exercise, solid spiritual guidance and support, probably the most effective curative intervention is a course of constitutional homeopathic treatment.

Manic phase symptoms:

- Elation, euphoria (some manic individuals are often irritable); delusions of grandeur
- High energy episodes
- Feelings of invincibility
- Less need for sleep
- Hallucinations in severe episodes
- Obsession with alcohol, spending money, sex, travel, gambling, shopping sprees
- Suspicion; perceiving others as a threat
- Refusal to accept their abnormal behavior; impaired reality testing

RECOMMENDED SUPPLEMENTS: *Manic Phase: Manic Depression Relief* (chewable tablets), *Brain Food, 5-HTP, Neuro Relaxer, L-Taurine, Grape Seed/ Skin Extract, Green Barley, GTF Chromium or 3-Chromium + Cinnamon Complex, Bone Density Calcium* and/or *Coral Calcium* (with magnesium and vitamin D), *Men's/Women's Ultimate Multiple Vitamin, Natural Lithium* from vegetable sources *(not the same as prescription Lithium salt).*

RECOMMENDED SUPPLEMENTS: *Depressive Phase: Depression Relief* (chewable tablets), *Brain Food, Royal Jelly, Neuro Complex, L-Taurine, Bone Density Calcium* (with magnesium and vitamin D), or *3-Chromium + Cinnamon Complex, Grape Seed/ Skin Extract, Choline/Inositol, Vitamin B-6, Men's/ Women's Ultimate Multiple Vitamin, 5-HTP* or *Neuro Relaxer* at bedtime, *Green Barley, Neuro Balancer* (take *Neuro Balancer* with food, one hour apart from other supplements), *Brain Igniter* (if needed for mental clarity), *Vitamin B Complex-50* and *DMG* (if needed).

Juvenile Bipolar Disorder

This deserves special attention because the presentation is usually quite different from the adult variety; often no periodicity of symptoms is discernable. A few of those with juvenile bipolar disorder may suffer from **pyroluria**, a genetic disorder causing abnormal production of **kryptopyrroles**, a waste product of hemoglobin synthesis which may worsen symptoms of depression. Improved diet and the recommended supplements

---

Note: Do not take additional *Choline-Inositol* or *Vanadium*. SAMe is not recommended simply because it is seldom effective.

address this problem. Some or all of the following symptoms characterize the disorder in children and teenagers:

- Persistent anxiety
- Irritability
- Uncontrolled anger, defiance, aggressive behavior, "affective storms"
- Impulsivity, lack of self-central, extreme willfulness
- Fearfulness, tendency to hide inner feelings from others
- Hypoglycemia
- Accumulation of copper in the brain
- Allergies, food and chemical sensitivities
- Cravings for carbohydrates or sweets
- Elevated lactic acid, especially in sedentary, overweight youngsters or those who consume a lot of sugar-laden foods
- Coated tongue with tiny red spots
- Apathy, fatigue
- Morning nausea
- Eyes sensitive to sunlight
- Stretch marks on skin
- Cold hands and feet
- Reduced head hair
- Thin finger nails with white spots on the nails
- Family history of mood disorders and/or alcoholism

RECOMMENDED SUPPLEMENTS: Take the following until symptoms go away. *Anxiety-Stress Relief* (chewable tablets), *Brain Food, Royal Jelly, Allergy Control* (1 or 2 tablets a day), *Neuro Complex, Vitamin B-6* (200mg twice a day), *Zinc Picolinate* (50mg, 1 capsule a day), *Men's/Women's Ultimate Multiple Vitamin* (1 capsule/tablet every 3 days), *DMG* (125mg 2 times a day), *L-Taurine* (500mg, 1 capsule a day) *Grape Seed/*

Skin Extract and *Green Barley*. If there is hypoglycemia, add *GTF Chromium* (200mcg, 1 tablet a day, as needed) or *3-Chromium + Cinnamon Complex*. *L-Carnosine* (500mg, 1 capsule every 3 days) should be taken to chelate copper.

If your child experiences low spirits and feelings of "depression" intermittently, she or he will recover after taking these supplements regularly. If supplementation and other suggested interventions do not suffice, or if your child feels suicidal, seek professional help.

Bible-based psychotherapy or counseling, combined with the above recommendations, have helped many people and may be necessary for the child and family in difficult cases.

From a Christian Perspective

Assuming for the moment that depression is neither profound nor prolonged, a lapse into depression presupposes a loss of spiritual perspective and faith. That is to say, if you didn't have depression before, it is difficult to succumb to depression of significant depth or duration if you maintain awareness of the overarching love, forgiveness, guidance, and presence of God, his son, the Lord Jesus, and the Holy Spirit in your life. Focus on what is *good* and *worthy* of praise. Don't focus on what's *wrong* and become consumed with a need to fix negative things. Speak to yourself in spiritual songs—filling your brain with beautiful music and lyrics (Ephesians 5: 10)—as music

---

Note: Consume plenty of green, orange, and yellow vegetables and fruits. Avoid artificial sweeteners and all forms of concentrated or refined sugars, as well as foods high in saturated fats. Avoid alcohol and caffeine. If your child needs a mood lift, fruits, vegetables, fermented soy products, soy yogurt, tempeh, or miso-nut tofu, brown rice, and legumes can help. If you notice that your youngster's mood deteriorates after eating wheat or other gluten-containing foods, add one capsule of *Super Enzymes Complex* in a meal containing gluten; or include in those glutinous meals organic cow's milk or yogurt made with soy, goat, or sheep milk.

has a positive effect on the brain and mood. Do you know that the indwelling Christ can give you peace in every situation? Feel His strong arms around you; let the peace of God fill your brain, body, and total being with His loving presence. Read Psalm 91 in the Bible and experience the supernatural place of safety and protection He provides (cf. Philippians 4:7). Frequent visits with friends and attending various social activities including Bible study meetings can keep you connected. When depression descends upon one of strong faith, it will usually be due to some disequilibrium in brain chemistry, possibly provoked by some adverse life circumstance. The supplements recommended can help your efforts to regain your equilibrium and spiritual vitality.

17. DIABETES MELLITUS

This describes body's inability to regulate glucose, the fuel used by cells to produce energy, and insulin—a hormone produced by the pancreas—that helps glucose enter cells. The normal range for glucose is between 70 and 100 milligrams per deciliter (mg/dl). A blood concentration of 140mg/dl or higher is considered diabetes.

Diabetes is often associated with a deep, resigned sadness, as though all the sweetness has gone out of life. For best results in overcoming diabetes, the underlying melancholy must be addressed, using strategies which are discussed throughout this book.

RECOMMENDED SUPPLEMENTS: *Glucose Metabolizer, 3 Chromium + Cinnamon Complex* or *GTF Chromium, Royal Jelly, Fenugreek/Thyme, Heart Prolongevity, Pure Advanced Gamma Vitamin E Complex, B-1, Women's/Men's Ultimate Multiple Vitamin, Grape Seed/ Skin Extract* or *Green Barley.* To reduce damage to the retina of the eyes, take *Healthy Eyes*. Monitor your blood sugar levels.

18. DRUG ADDICTION or Substance Dependence

Whether legal or illegal, habitual overuse of substances in excess to get some desired effect is dependence. You may build up tolerance to a substance, thus needing an ever-increasing amount to produce the desired effect or prevent withdrawal. Whether the substance is injected, taken orally, or inhaled, addictive substances can, to varying degrees, influence the brain, mind, and body. Cocaine, heroin, methadone, diazepam (Valium), phenobarbital, alcohol, marijuana, rohypnol ("roofies"), gamma-hydroxy-butyrate (GHB), and numerous potentially dangerous drugs are abused, causing users untold miseries and sometimes death.

If you are severely addicted to barbiturates, anti-anxiety drugs, cocaine, or heroin, you need to be under a doctor's supervision to taper off gradually. Participate in a Christian support group or Christian psychotherapeutic halfway house. You may need a 12-step self-help program, biofeedback/neuro-feedback or behavioral therapy. Learn to identify your "weakness" or "triggers." For example, don't go to places where you are tempted; instead go to places that honor God. Pray for the Holy Spirit's power to overcome the desire for substances that destroy your brain.

RECOMMENDED SUPPLEMENTS: *Brain Food, Royal Jelly, Neuro Relaxer, Addiction Relief* (chewable tablets), *Clarimen GC* (Creatine Monohydrate), *Grape Seed/Skin Extract, 5-HTP* at bedtime, *Neuro Balancer, Men's/Women's Ultimate Multiple Vitamin, Allergy Control, Immune Enhancer I* and *II, Liver Detoxifier and Regenerator, L-Glutamine, L-Carnosine, Heart Prolongevity, Body Pure Colon Cleanse, and Vitamin C* (500mg—taken twice a day). Consume a well-balanced natural food diet; add cooked Kudzu at least once a week to your food. If you suffer seizures as a result of phencyclidine (PCP) withdrawal, take *Seizure Relief* (chewable tablets) and see a doctor. If you suffer insomnia, see recommendations under that heading. God can take away destructive cravings and give you a passion for becoming like His Son. (See also Alcoholism.)

19. FATIGUE, LOW ENERGY, AND LOW VITALITY

Low energy can be caused by chronic stress that disturbs psychological, mental, spiritual, and social balance. The chronic stresses of daily living can cause excessive production of cortisol, causing fatigue and a variety of other symptoms. Chronic stress can deplete nutrients, so follow the general dietary instructions at the beginning of this chapter.

In addition, hereditary factors, poor diet, inadequate or unrefreshing sleep, depression, and a wide variety of illnesses can negatively affect energy level. Refer to specific conditions elsewhere in this chapter for help with low energy due to illness.

RECOMMENDED SUPPLEMENTS: *Royal Jelly, L-Carnosine, Maca, L-Glutamine, Men's/Women's Ultimate Multiple Vitamin, Immune Enhancer I* and *II, Ester C, or Vitamin C (500 or 1,000 with bioflavonoids), Vitamin B-6, DMG, Heart Prolongevity* or *CoQ10,* and *Astragalus.*

20. FIBROMYALGIA, BODY PAIN, FATIGUE

SYMPTOMS—chronic fatigue; pain in muscles, ligaments, joints and tendons; morning stiffness; headaches; sleep abnormalities; mood changes; sensitivity to light and noise; anxiety in anticipation of emotional stress, worry and pain; depression, difficulty focusing and concentrating; restless leg syndrome; sleep apnea and bruxism. Most people with fibromyalgia also suffer from brain chemical disturbances. Many experience disturbed sleep characterized by interruption of normal sleep brain wave activity by episodes of wakeful brain wave activity. All of these symptoms can impede spiritual growth.

CAUSES—Fibromyalgia has hereditary or genetic origins and can be precipitated by acute illness, trauma, or immune dysfunction. It is often associated with Epstein-Barr Virus infection (EBV) and Chronic Fatigue Syndrome (CFS).

DIAGNOSIS—As the medical profession has slowly taken fibromyalgia more seriously as a diagnostic entity, diagnostic criteria have emerged that are somewhat arbitrary and exclusive. The most reliable physical finding in fibromyalgia is the existence of specific trigger points, an array of tender spots in the musculature, the locations of which are surprisingly consistent with the findings of the American College of Rheumatology. Of course, a diagnosis of fibromyalgia is based upon the exclusion of other disorders. Lab tests and imaging procedures are becoming more useful in the diagnosis.

TREATMENT

The *nutritional* goal is to correctly nourish the immune system and assist the body to recover from the deranging force that caused the imbalance. Wholesome balanced eating is important. As you recover, increase exercise as tolerated.

RECOMMENDED SUPPLEMENTS: *Immune Enhancers I* and *II* if immune system is compromised; *Royal Jelly, Astragalus Root* is a powerful immune booster multiplying your T-cells, macrophages and Natural Killer (NK) cells. It is included in *Super Immune Enhancer II*. Also take *Grape Seed/Skin Extract; Brain Food* and *Brain Igniter* (lower priced and better than SAMe), *Neuro Complex* and *Neuro Balancer* (if depression is present); *Heart Prolongevity* is added after two or three weeks (one or two a day) for boosting tissue oxygenation, blood flow and immune functions. This supplement includes *Co-Enzyme*

Q10, Alpha Lipoic Acid, L-Carnatine and much more; *5-HTP* or *Natural Sleep* supplement is added two capsules at bedtime. You may need additional supplementation if restful sleep eludes you despite *5-HTP* and/or *Natural Sleep; Magnesium Citrate* 500mg and *Malic acid* one or more times daily has shown to relieve pain and discomfort. Take these supplements with food. If you have difficulty swallowing pills, you may take the *Complete Nutritional Mix;* homeopathic medicines are very effective when prescribed by a trained homeopath. Other supplements that may be indicated are *Liver Detoxifier and Regenerator, Allergy Control,* and *Esiak; Allergy Control* if you suffer allergies; biofeedback/neuro-feedback with cognitive behavioral therapy have been effective in the management of fibromyalgia.

DIETARY AND OTHER LIFESTYLE RECOMMENDATIONS

- Do not take supplements every day for more than one month; skip two or three days a week and take only as needed. More is not necessarily better. After complete recovery, take supplements only as needed for maintenance.
- Avoid colas, white flour, processed foods, refined carbohydrates, and sugar. Instead use xylitol.
- Get plenty of rest.
- Drink plenty of filtered or steam-distilled water.
- Eat steamed vegetables, rather than raw, unless they are organically grown.
- Eat a balanced diet of natural foods rich in vegetables.
- Install a shower filter.
- Exercise regularly—stretching, walking, swimming, more vigorous as tolerated—if your health permits.

21. GENERAL HEALTH

See the early section of this chapter.

RECOMMENDED SUPPLEMENTS: As needed: *Men's/ Women's Ultimate Multiple Vitamin, Royal Jelly, Heart Prolongevity, Clarimen GC* (Creatine Monohydrate*), Ester-C* (chewable lozenges or tablets), *Immune Enhancer I & Immune Enhancer II* and *Royal Jelly.* Take some or all the above supplements in maintenance dosages or intermittently if no illness is present. If you are constantly tired, sleepy, and have no energy, take recommended supplements in section 19, Fatigue, Low Energy and Low Vitality (e.g. once or twice per week).

22. HEART/ARTERIOSCHLEROSIS

Cerebrovascular (brain blood vessels) and cardiovascular (heart blood vessels) disorders progress slowly, resulting in narrowed, inflexible blood vessels. Usually, what is true of the heart is true of the brain. Until other new advances come along such as gene therapy, blood stem cell therapies, genetically engineered medicines to reduce plaque and tissue-engineering, these supplements can keep your heart healthy. Healthy diet, regular exercise, positive attitude, and overcoming negative emotions such as resentment are integral parts of any regimen to restore and maintain heart, brain, and vascular health. Dietary fiber is good to protect the heart also.

RECOMMENDED SUPPLEMENTS: *Heart Prolongevity, Brain Food, EDTA Oral Chelation* capsules, *Advanced Gamma Vitamin E, Royal Jelly, Green Barley, Grape Seed/Skin Extract, L-Taurine, Hawthorn Berry, Magnesium Citrate, Super Enzyme Complex, GTF Chromium* and/or *3 Chromium + Cinnamon Complex* (alternate between the two every other week), and *Biotin.*

23. HORMONE IMBALANCE IN WOMEN

Women can naturally balance their hormones. Bio-identical hormones can help reduce hot flashes, fatigue, insomnia, lower the risk of osteoporosis, heart disease, and maximize the quality of life. Studies show that progesterone is the first hormone to deplete in most women. Deficiency symptoms include PMS, hot flashes, night sweats, mood swings, and miscarriages. Regular hormone testing is important to determine your specific need. Saliva testing appears to be the most accurate for determining hormone levels because saliva measures only levels of active hormones. The safest estrogen is estriol. Estrone and estradiol are toxic forms of estrogen. Estriol can reverse vaginal atrophy, increase cervical mucus, and reduce hot flashes and sweating. A five-year prospective study of estriol therapy revealed that this treatment was successful in 92 percent of cases (*Horm Metab Res.* (Nov. 1987): 19:11:579–84.

According to Jonathan V. Wright, MD, who pioneered the use of many bioidentical hormones, replacement dosages fluctuate considerably among individual women. He also adds that supplementation should follow the same monthly cycles as estrogen. ***Note:*** Women with estrogen receptor-positive breast cancer should stay away from any form of estrogen to avoid stimulating tumor growth.

Testosterone is essential for women's ovaries and adrenal glands at about one tenth the level as in men. Testosterone steadily declines from around the age of 30 and some post menopausal women may have very low testosterone. If you suspect imbalance in your hormones, find a doctor who is skilled and knowledgeable to measure and give you the correct level of hormones. You also need to be monitored from time to time through urine, saliva, or a blood test.

RECOMMENDED SUPPLEMENTS: *L-Carnosine, Royal Jelly, Women's Ultimate Multiple Vitamin, Hormone Balancer* (for

balancing female hormones—one every other day for mainte-
nance), *Progesterone Cream* (plant derived), *Immune Enhancer
I & II, Astragalus, Choline-Inositol, Advanced Gamma Vitamin
E Complex, Super Enzyme Complex, 3 Chromium + Cinnamon
Complex, Silica, Bone Density Calcium* (with magnesium and
vitamin D), *Maca, 7-Keto (DHEA), Hot Flashes Relief* (chewable tablets). *Neuro Relaxer* helps to reduce anxiety. *Add Green
Barley.* Other hormones, after tests. Stop caffeine and alcohol.
Note: Exercise regularly. Eat a high fiber diet and about two
ounces of *fermented soy products*, including miso, tempeh, and
soy yogurt. Ground flaxseed (not oil) in moderation is beneficial. Most people will not need more than 500 milligrams of
Evening Primrose Oil a day as it may cause bleeding.

24. IMMUNE DYSFUNCTION

Restoring, protecting, and maintaining a healthy immune
system is vital to health and well-being. Make sure your diet includes plenty of fruits, vegetables, whole grains, and adequate
protein. Of course, regular exercise is also important, as is
adequate sleep.

RECOMMENDED SUPPLEMENTS: *Immune Enhancer
I* and/or *Immune Enhancer II, Women's/Men's Ultimate Mul-
tiple Vitamin, Royal Jelly, Heart Prolongevity* (or *L-Carnitine,
CoQ10), Grape Seed/Skin Extract, 7-Keto, Selenium, Advanced
Gamma Vitamin E Complex, Green Barley, Liver Detoxifier and
Regenerator* (one capsule a day for maintenance).

25. HYPOGLYCEMIA

As glucose fluctuates in the brain, so do our moods. Eat six *or*
more small meals consisting of complex carbohydrates (whole
grains) and vegetables or high protein foods and vegetables.
Avoid sugar and other refined carbohydrates; eschew artificial

sweeteners. Minimize fruit juices. Use xylitol, erythritol, or other natural sweeteners with low glycemic index in moderation. Regular exercise, stress reduction, and adequate sleep will also reduce hypoglycemic symptoms.

RECOMMENDED SUPPLEMENTS: *GTF Chromium* or *3 Chromium + Cinnamon Complex, Royal Jelly, Glucose Metabolizer, Clarimen GC* (Creatine Monohydrate), *Pure Psyllium Husk with Apple Pectin, Men's/Women's Ultimate Multiple Vitamin, Bone Density Calcium* (with magnesium and vitamin D*).*

26. INSOMNIA

Sleep disorders—difficulty falling asleep, waking repeatedly, waking up too early, shallow or restless sleep—can affect people of any age, but prevalence increases with advancing years primarily due to reduced melatonin secretion by the pineal gland. Occasional insomnia is not uncommon. Persistent insomnia creates relentless misery and compromises health and body functions globally. Regular deep sleep is necessary for body repair and regeneration. Insomnia may be due to primary dysfunction of sleep-regulating mechanisms within and/or outside the brain; or it may be secondary to organ or system dysfunction—heart, liver, brain, pancreas, kidneys, prostate, thyroid, or adrenals; endocrine, digestive, respiratory, or autonomic nervous systems. At some point in its course, almost any disease may disturb sleep. Anxiety, worry, excessive stress, grieving, depression, allergies, pain, medications, poor diet, lack of exercise, lack of sunlight, and a host of environmental factors may cause or contribute to disturbance of sleep. These underlying conditions must be addressed. Refer to other conditions in this chapter as appropriate to your needs.

AVOID caffeine, tobacco, chocolate, sauerkraut, bacon, ham, tomatoes, and eggplant within three hours of going to bed. Some of these contain tyramine, which increases release of norepinephrine and histamine, both of which are stimulants capable of disrupting sleep.

RECOMMENDED SUPPLEMENTS: Daytime: Take *Male* or *Femal Performance Support, Royal Jelly, Men's/Women's Ultimate Multiple Vitamin* and *L-Carnosine*. Include *Neuro Balancer* (taken with food separately from other supplements during daytime) if insomnia is accompanied by depression. Nighttime: Take in the following order: *Natural 5-HTP (50 to 400mg) and Bone Density Calcium* (with magnesium and vitamin D) or *Coral Calcium Plus* (both of these 30 minutes before bedtime), *Neuro Relaxer* (2 capsules with dinner), *Natural Sleep* (3 capsules at bedtime), *L-Taurine, B-6, Insomnia Relief* tablets (3 tablets at bedtime), *Anxiety and Stress Relief* tablets (chewable)—before exercising, and *Melatonin* (if you are younger than thirty years of age, don't take Melatonin more than 10 days in a row). Get enough sunlight because it increases production of melatonin. *Note:* Deep within the brain in the anterior hypothalamus lies a cluster of thousands of neurons called the *suprachiasmatic nucleus* (SCN), which regulates the body's circadian rhythms. This is powered by light via the retina of the eye. When light reaches the retina, neural signals are generated and travel to the SCN via a neural pathway called the retinohypothalamic tract. The pineal gland produces the hormone *melatonin*. Small percentages of the serotonin and 5-hydroxytryptophan (5-HTP), present in other parts of the brain, combine to produce more melatonin. In sum, when the sun goes down, melatonin levels go up.

27. MEMORY

For more information see under *Brain Fog*.

The supplements below have shown to promote new brain cell growth, improve short- and long-term memory; prevent dementias; reduce ADHD symptoms, enhance memory and concentration, improve concentration, learning and other cognitive functions; reduce anxiety, depression, brain fatigue and stress and protect the brain from toxins.

RECOMMENDED SUPPLEMENTS: *Brain Food, Brain Igniter, Neuro Complex, Royal Jelly, L-Carnosine, Male* or *Female Performance Support* (if testosterone level is low), *Neuro Balancer, Neuro Relaxer* (Take two with dinner if you have difficulty falling asleep), *5-HTP* at bedtime, *DMAE.* After 1 to 2 months, take *Immune Enhancer I & II, Vitamin B-1* and *Heart Prolongevity,* and *Clarimen GC* (Creatine Monohydrate), to prevent hardening of the arteries.

28. MENOPAUSE PROBLEMS

Petal Soft contains many phytochemicals designed to balance estrogens, and progesterone in your body to reduce the level of 16, a-hydroxyestrone, known to promote cancer.

RECOMMENDED SUPPLEMENTS: *Hormone Balancer* (one capsule a day), *Progesterone Cream, Black Cohosh* (One 500mg capsule a day or as needed for hot flashes), *Women's Ultimate Multiple Vitamin, Hormone Imbalance Relief* (chewable tablets), *GTF Chromium* or *3-Chromium + Cinnamon Complex.* If you are overweight or afflicted with insomnia or yeast infection, see those conditions in this chapter. See also Hormone Imbalances. GLA or primrose oil should be taken in moderation because it can interfere with the blood-clotting mechanism and cause bleeding in women; discontinue if you have excessive bleeding. Ask your health care provider to test your hormones to maintain healthy levels.

29. MOOD LIFTERS

Read also information under "Depression."

RECOMMENDED SUPPLEMENTS: *Neuro Complex, Men's/Women's Ultimate Multiple Vitamin, Royal Jelly, GTF Chromium* or *3-Chromium + Cinnamon Complex, 5-HTP* at bedtime. *Neuro Balancer* (1 tablet in the mid-morning with snack). You may need *Maca*.

30. MULTIPLE SCLEROSIS

Multiple Sclerosis results from the gradual destruction of myelin, a fatty substance that forms a protective sheath on nerve fibers (axons). The myelin coating of axons permits normal nerve transmissions. As myelin in the brain and spinal cord is replaced by plaques and scar tissue, nerve transmission is slowed and disrupted. Initially this degenerative process affects primarily motor nerves; as the disease progresses, sensory and other types of neurons are increasingly affected.

Muscular symptoms include weakness, leg dragging, clumsiness, fatigue, tingling, dizziness, slurred speech, spasms, and stiffness. The course of the disease is extremely variable, making it difficult to predict.

Visual symptoms include pain in the eyeball, blurred or double vision, or progressive loss of vision.

Sensory symptoms include sensations of pins-and-needles, electrical currents, heaviness, and numbness in the arms and legs.

Gastrointestinal symptoms include indigestion, loss of bowel sensations, nausea, gastric reflux, and vomiting.

Vestibular symptoms include light-headedness, sensation of drunkenness, or vertigo.

Genitourinary symptoms include incontinence, loss of bladder sensation, loss of sexual desire, and impotence.

Treatment Tips Most impressive is *Hyperbaric Oxygen Therapy* (HBOT). Researchers theorize that oxygen delivery to nerve tissues can relieve symptoms without serious side effects. Dr.

Richard Neubauer of Ocean Medical Center near Ft. Lauderdale, Florida, is perhaps the leading authority on HBOT. According to Dr. Neubauer, 70–80 percent of his MS patients show improvement with HBO therapy. HBOT delivers oxygen to every cell in the body; this stabilizes the disease and stops the progressive deterioration. Dr. Neubauer reports that low pressure HBO of 1.3–1.5 atmospheres produces the best results. The chamber's atmospheric pressure increases the number of molecules of oxygen dissolved in the blood.

Dietary Recommendations

- Consume low-fat, unprocessed whole grains, vegetables, legumes, nuts, seeds, and fruits—preferably organically grown.
- Eat fiber-rich foods like whole grains, fruits, and vegetables and bran, apple pectin, psyllium seed husk or ground flax seeds. Eliminate refined sugars and processed foods. Use only a small amount of pure maple syrup, honey, or molasses if you must; xylitol or stevia are better sweeteners. Drink pure water. Avoid margarine, all trans-fatty acids, and minimize saturated fats.

RECOMMENDED SUPPLEMENTS: *MS Relief* (chewable tablets), *Grape Seed/ Skin Extract, Brain Food, Choline-Inositol, Royal Jelly, Pure Enzyme Complex, Men's/Women's Ultimate Multiple Vitamin, Bone Density Calcium, Royal Jelly, Healthy Eyes* and *Immune Enhancers I and II.* Seek an experienced holistic physician to recommend further supplementation and other natural interventions.

31. NARCOLEPSY

Narcolepsy is a syndrome that appears to be caused by neurobiological imbalance that interferes with the brain's ability to regulate normal sleep-wake cycles. A person with narcolepsy may experience a combination of symptoms including:

1. episodes of deep sleep from which he or she can be aroused only with great difficulty, often coming on suddenly without warning;
2. muscle weakness or cataplexy;
3. sleep paralysis in which the person cannot move any part of the body for a few minutes or longer;
4. auditory or visual hallucinations, called hypnagogic phenomena.

Conventional treatment: Usually tricyclics, selective serotonin reuptake inhibitors, Adderall, Ritalin, Tofranil or Modafranil are prescribed to control narcolepsy.

RECOMMENDED SUPPLEMENTS: *Neuro Complex, Royal Jelly, Brain Food, L-Glutamine, Adrenal Support, L-Tyrosine, GTF Chromium* or *3 Chromium + Cinnamon Complex, Royal Jelly, Bone Density Calcium* (with magnesium and vitamin D), *Choline/Inosital, GTF Chromium, Men's/Women's Ultimate Multiple Vitamin, Immune Enhancer I* and *II, Liver Detoxifier and Regenerator* for those who use any kind of prescription or non-prescription drugs. This nutritional protocol keeps blood sugar levels relatively even through the day to sustain wakefulness. To enhance sleep, *5-HTP, Vitamin B-6* and/or *Neuro Relaxer* (2 capsules 30 minutes before bedtime). Also, *L-Carnosine* and other supplements maintain normal production of norepinephrine to keep the sympathetic nervous system active to maintain alertness. See instructions for healthy eating in Chapter 8.

32. OBSESSIVE-COMPULSIVE DISORDER (OCD)

Only in recent years have scientists come to understand clearly one of the mechanisms of obsessive thoughts and compulsive behavior: neurobiochemical imbalances or deficiencies in the brain. Christians also suffer from OCD and endure unnecessary suffering due to lack of understanding of the spiritual and physiological issues. To present to Christians with OCD (what I wrote earlier about John and Joyce) can only induce withdrawal, anxiety, guilt, fear, and so on. Conventional treatment utilizes drugs like Prozac and other SSRIs, often in higher doses for OCD than those prescribed for depression. Sometimes Anafranil (a tricyclic antidepressant) or Buspar (an anti-anxiety agent) may be prescribed. These drugs are variably effective and invariably toxic.

RECOMMENDED SUPPLEMENTS: At bedtime, *Methionine, Bone Density Calcium* (with magnesium and vitamin D), *Vitamin C (Time Release), Vitamin B-6* and *Men's/Women's Ultimate Multiple Vitamin.* Do not take additional *Vitamin B-Complex, Vitamin, B-12* or *folic acid* beyond what is in the multiple vitamins. Some will need *Choline-Inositol.* If you have experienced positive results from SSRI's in the past, the above program should work well for you.

33. OBESITY

Tips for Weight Loss:
The key is to balance energy expenditure and food consumption. Apart from serious genetic and hormonal factors predisposing to pathological weight gain, most overweight people can lose weight by controlling the quantity of food eaten, combined with a regimen of regular exercise. Deficiencies of DHEA, thyroid, and other hormones have been associated with obesity as well as many age-related conditions such as rheumatoid arthritis, increased pro-inflammatory cytokines and interleukin-6, chilliness or heat intolerance, and sleep disturbance. Ask your doctor to test your levels of various hormones.

1. Eat slowly and keep the food in the mouth, chewing as long as possible.
2. If you have an irresistible urge to eat junk food, keep it in the mouth long enough to taste it, and then spit it out. Rather than eating for comfort, go for a walk, preferably with a dear friend; sing to lift your spirits; pray and give your troubles to God, and seek solace from the Supreme Comforter.
3. When you eat sweet foods, drink water immediately after to reduce the sugar craving. See also Drugs/Substance Abuse for strategies to kick the sugar addiction.
4. Eat several small meals a day rather than the basic three meals. Remember that the stomach is about the size of your fist, usually a volume of 1½ to 2 cups. Eating more than two cups of food per meal is overeating.
5. When your stomach is not full, pull it inward toward your spine. Take time to breathe fully.
6. Avoid unhealthy buffets. With a fixed price, you'll be tempted to eat a lot to get the most for your money.
7. Make a list when shopping for food. Check it twice to eliminate junk food items!
8. Exercise regularly as appropriate for the status of your health.
9. Avoid appetite-suppressing drugs. Their serious side effects are numerous, including addictive potential, impairment of memory and concentration, palpitations, anxiety, insomnia, liver damage, and heart attack.
10. A few computer assisted biofeedback or neuro-feedback sessions have been found effective for some people. Make sure you record a session for repeated listening at home.

RECOMMENDED SUPPLEMENTS: *Weight Loss Trio* (three bottles): 1.) *Weight Regulator*, 2.) *7-Keto (DHEA)*, 3.)

Super Enzymes Complex, Male or Female Performance Enhancer (for men), *Royal Jelly* and *L-Cysteine*. Reduce use of *Super Enzymes Complex* after 3 months. Also, *GTF Chromium* and/or *3 Chromium + Cinnamon Complex* (alternate the chromiums every other week), *Natural 5-HTP, L-Taurine, CLA, Men's/Women's Ultimate Multiple Vitamin*.

34. PANIC ATTACKS OR PHOBIAS (See Also Anxiety)

RECOMMENDED SUPPLEMENTS: *Neuro Balancer, Neuro Relaxer,* (some may need *Cool and Calm,* 1 or 2 capsules with meals), *Neuro Complex, 5HTP* at bedtime, *Men's/Women's Ultimate Multiple Vitamin,* and *Panic Attack Relief* (chewable tablets). Some individuals may need *L-Tyrosine, 3 Chromium + Cinnamon Complex* and *L-Glutamine*. Some may require supplements especially formulated for them. Take *Neuro Balancer* with food, separate from other supplements.

35. PREMENSTRUAL SYNDROME (PMS), DYSMEN-ORRHEA (Cramps)

RECOMMENDED SUPPLEMENTS: *Hormone Balancer, Royal Jelly, PMS Relief* (chewable tablets*), Women's Ultimate Multiple Vitamin, Vitamin B-6, Natural 5-HTP* at bedtime, *Bone Density Calcium* (with magnesium and vitamin D). Eat pineapple. If you experience depression, see section on depression. If you are constipated, use *Body Detox /Colon Cleanse,* and/or *Constipation Relief* (chewable tablets), drink plenty of pure water (preferably warm), get plenty of exercise, and eat a healthy, balanced diet. GLA's such as borage oil, black currant oil, or *Super Evening Primrose Oil* should be taken with caution, due to potentially hazardous effects if used excessively by susceptible individuals.

36. SCHIZOPHRENIA and SCHIZO-PHRENIFORM DISORDERS

Scientists have not found common brain or functioning specific to schizophrenia, related disorders, or psychoses involving a breakdown of reality testing, such as hallucinations or delusions. In a condition called schizoaffective disorder, symptoms of both bipolar disorder and schizophrenia occur. Psychosis with schizophreniform symptoms occurs in many brain disorders, including dementia and delirium. Caution: adolescents who may be showing early signs of personality disorders, anxiety, and depression may be mistaken for early schizophrenic symptoms, resulting in inappropriate treatment. For someone experiencing psychotic episodes, psychiatrists usually prescribe the following drugs known as a second generation drugs: Risperdal, Zyprexa, Seroquel, Geodon, or Abilify. Giving a patient more than one antipsychotic drug at a time is not recommended. Of course it is ideal to intervene with natural remedies early while symptoms are mild and more readily yield to gentler treatment.

RECOMMENDED SUPPLEMENTS: *Schizophrenia Relief* (chewable tablets), *Neuro Complex, L-Methionine, Vitamin B-50 Complex, Brain Food, L-Glutamine* and *Men's/Women's Ultimate Multiple Vitamin. If* there is *frequent catatonia, violent outbursts, delusions or hallucinations,* add *Neuro Balancer* (take *Neuro Balancer* with food, separately from other supplements), *5-HTP, and Neuro Relaxer* (one or two capsules at bedtime). When symptoms improve and stabilize, add *Brain Igniter* (one capsule once a week). *Brain Igniter,* along with *Brain Food,* and *Schizophrenia Relief* (chewable tablets), targets nerve receptors in the prefrontal cortex and hippocampus. Neuro Complex may prevent the slow tendency to cerebral cortex atrophy sometimes seen in those afflicted with schizophrenia. Some people may need a specifically formulated supplement protocol.

37. SEIZURE DISORDERS/EPILEPSY

RECOMMENDED SUPPLEMENTS: *Epilepsy Relief* (chewable tablets), *L-Taurine, L-Tyrosine, Liver Detoxifier and Regenerator, Men's/Women's Ultimate Multiple Vitamin* (1 Capsule, 3 mornings per week), *Neuro Relaxer, L-Glycine, L-Glutamine, Natural 5-HTP, Gotu Cola, Bone Density Calcium* (with magnesium and vitamin D), and *DMG*. Cook with ginger root. Long-term use of anti-seizure or epilepsy medications can lead to biotin deficiency. All are quite toxic and should be avoided; however, these drugs should be gradually withdrawn under the supervision of an experienced holistic physician.

38. SEXUAL ADDICTION

Avoid the habit of indulging in pornography. We must oppose the evil of prurient sexual interest by recruiting the power of God. We are called upon to guard against such satanic intrusions. Inclinations to engage in any activity that rejects Christ-likeness should be yielded to the fullness of the Holy Spirit. Our interests and activities should be guided by scriptural teachings, not based on our sinful impulses (Eph. 6:12). Buy the author's cassette tape, filled with liberating, spirit-filled images for your brain and mind transformation, made available from Integrative Medicine and Biofeedback Clinic. Don't take testosterone, *Male or Female Performance Support*, DHEA, pregnenolone (unless your blood levels of these hormones are low), *Maca*, or extra B-vitamins (except what's in multiple vitamins). Reduce or eliminate animal flesh from your diet; increase spiritual activities, exercise or do hard physical work.

RECOMMENDED SUPPLEMENTS: *5-HTP* at bedtime, and afternoon, *Neuro Relaxer (2 with dinner), Methionine, Vitamin B6, Ester C, Bone Density Calcium* (with magnesium and vitamin D), *Choline-Inositol, L-Taurine* and *Cool and Calm.*

39. SMOKING RELIEF

If you find smoking pleasant and relaxing, stop smoking and find other activities to compensate. If you smoke when you feel angry about something—pray and forgive—allow Christ's love to saturate you. For energy and to stimulate your brain and body—use recommended supplements, exercise regularly, and eat well. Biofeedback or neuro-feedback with transforming behavioral messages can do wonders. The most effective way to quit is cold turkey while you are taking the supplements and managing your anxiety, stress and other issues in life with the power of God.

RECOMMENDED SUPPLEMENTS: *Heart Prolongevity, Royal Jelly, Smoking Relief* (chewable tablets), *Liver Detoxified and Regenerator, Men's/Women's Ultimate Multiple Vitamin, DMG, Neuro Balancer, Neuro Complex, Neuro Relaxer, L-Carnatine Liquid* (1 teaspoon), or smoked fruit drops to compensate urge.

40. SOCIAL PHOBIA (See also Anxiety)

Bible-based Christian counseling is recommended.

RECOMMENDED SUPPLEMENTS: *Social Phobia Relief* (chewable tablets), *5-HTP* at bedtime, *Brain Food, Neuro Complex, GTF Chromium* or *3-Chromium + Cinnamon Complex, Men's/Women's Ultimate Multiple Vitamin,* and *Tyrosine.*

41. STRESS

RECOMMENDED SUPPLEMENTS: *L-Carnosine,* Men's/Women's Ultimate Multiple Vitamin, Royal Jelly, Stress Relief* (chewable tablets), *Neuro Complex, Neuro Relaxer* (if unable to relax), *Neuro Balancer* (if accompanied by anxiety or depression), *Heart Prolongevity, DMG, CoQ1O* (if not taking *Heart*

Prolongevity) and *Maca.* Exercise and diet are important. See discussion earlier in Chapter Four. See Anxiety and Depression if applicable.

42. THYROID

HYPOTHYROIDISM. Characterized by insufficient production of thyroid hormones, it is actually a constellation of diseases of various etiologies. The severity of the symptoms depends on the level of thyroid hormones, though there is not always a simple linear correlation between numbers and severity of symptoms. Symptoms are variable and include apathy, fatigue, impaired memory, mental dullness, weight gain, slow heart rate, thinning of hair mass, dry skin, constipation, puffiness of face with dull expression, anemia, low basal temperature, and inability to tolerate cold. Laboratory determination of circulating thyroid hormone levels and anti-thyroid antibodies is important. However, people with normal thyroid levels may still suffer many hypothyroid symptoms.

Clearly there are subtleties and complexities of thyroid function that have eluded medical science. So the diagnosis must be made on the basis of lab results and symptoms. If there is an autoimmune component driving your hypothyroidism, see supplement recommendations in Immune Dysfunction section. Wholesome balanced eating is important, especially including frequent consumption of sea vegetables which are rich in iodine and other minerals needed for optimum thyroid function. Avoid eating raw cabbage, rutabagas, spinach, and radishes, all of which inhibit synthesis of thyroid hormones. It should be emphasized that unless the condition is severe and unremitting, it can usually be treated naturally without resorting to thyroid hormone replacement. It is best to intervene early with the resources God has provided for our sustenance and healing.

RECOMMENDED SUPPLEMENTS: *Thyroid Health* (unnecessary if you are eating sea vegetables generously every day), *Vitamin* B6, Tyrosine, and *Men's/Women's Ultimate Multiple Vitamin.*

HYPERTHYROIDISM. Characterized by overproduction of thyroid hormones, an even more diverse array of diseases is subsumed under the diagnosis of hyperthyroidism than we find in hypothyroidism. One of these is called thyroid storm—fortunately not common; it has a sudden onset of life-threatening symptoms; with the exception of thyroid storm, most cases of hyperthyroidism are amenable to natural treatment strategies, particularly if treatment is begun early before symptoms become intense. Common signs and symptoms include goiter, tachycardia, tremor, various eye symptoms, atrial fibrillation, nervousness, increased activity, increased sweating, heat intolerance, palpitations, fatigue, increased appetite, weight loss, insomnia, weakness, and frequent bowel movements.

RECOMMENDED SUPPLEMENTS: *Hyperthyroid Relief* (chewable tablets). Eat thyroxine-blocking foods such as cabbage, broccoli, rutabagas, spinach, and radishes. *Avoid* sea vegetables because they contain iodine.

43. TOURETTE'S SYNDROME

Avoid sugar, alcohol, and caffeine; drink herb teas, coffee substitutes made from roasted cereal grains, roasted dandelion root, and/or roasted chicory.

RECOMMENDED SUPPLEMENTS: *Tourette's Symptom Relief* (chewable tablets), *Neuro Relaxer* (Take 1 *Neuro Relaxer* capsule between breakfast and lunch and 1 at bedtime), *5HTP* at bedtime with *Tourette's Symptom Relief* (chewable tablets), *Men's/Women's Ultimate Multiple Vitamin, Brain Food* (Take 1 to 2 daily), *Cool and Calm* (1 capsule with lunch and dinner).

44. VERTIGO

Vertigo is usually caused by dysfunction of the vestibular system in the inner ear. When this system is disordered by trauma, inflammation, or disease, the sense of balance is compromised. Vertigo is the sensation of spinning or rolling, often accompanied by nausea.

RECOMMENDED SUPPLEMENTS: *Vertigo Relief* (chewable tablets), *Brain Food, Royal Jelly, Vitamin B-12, DMG, Allergy Control, Choline/Inositol, Brain Igniter,* and *Bone Density Calcium* (with Magnesium and Vitamin D). If you suffer from nausea, use *Nausea Relief* (chewable tablets); or try ginger root capsules or fresh ginger with lemon and honey tea.

RECOMMENDED COMBINATIONS FOR BALANCING THE BRAIN NATURALLY

- Doses recommended are for persons age 16 and over. For younger children, use one quarter of the recommended doses or use your discretion.
- If possible, eat a well-balanced diet of organically grown foods. Eat fiber-rich foods like whole grains, vegetables, and fruits; and add a small amount of bran, apple pectin, psyllium seed husk or ground flax seeds as needed to maintain good bowel function.
- Hyperbaric oxygen therapy, intravenous hydrogen peroxide therapy, chelation and ozone or other oxidation therapies can work miracles *in difficult cases.*
- Exercise regularly to keep your body and brain active.
- Breathing correctly is important. Every breath can clean your mind and energize your body and help you manage your stress better. More information can be obtained from ***www.natureshospital.com*** under "Breathing."

- Eliminate refined sugars, white flour, soft drinks, and processed foods. Use only a small amount of pure xylitol, erythritol, stevia, maple syrup, honey, or molasses as sweetener. Avoid artificial sweeteners.
- Maintain a healthy blood glucose level.
- Eat live-culture yogurt or take acidophilus or an intestinal flora supplement.
- Avoid margarine and all trans-fatty acids. Use a small amount of grape seed oil, coconut oil or olive oil for cooking.
- Get plenty of sleep. Most adults need eight hours; children need ten hours per night.
- Drink pure water, at least one-half ounce per pound of body weight daily, more when perspiring freely.
- Keep in mind that some people who take these supplements will experience dramatic improvement immediately. Others may take several weeks or months or longer if they suffer from chronic or degenerative disorders.
- Don't give up! Even if you don't feel perfect, keep smiling, praying, loving, doing good, and maintaining your creative spark.

SAFETY OF RECOMMENDED SUPPLEMENTS

All the supplements recommended for various conditions are safe, especially compared to prescription medications. They are composed of vitamins, minerals, enzymes, amino acids, oils, and extracts from herbs, vegetables, and fruits.

An excellent source for obtaining supplements of the highest purity, potency, quality and efficacy is *Nature's Hospital.* Many of the supplements herein recommended are proprietary blends available only through Nature's Hospital. Their products are manufactured in FDA-approved laboratories which received an "A" rating for overall GMP (Good Manufacturing Practices) from the Natural Nutritional Food Association (NNFA).

Identifying the right supplements or natural medicine for your needs is not difficult. When you determine your condition (e.g., brain fog), you can determine what supplements can help those with brain fog. By employing the appropriate supplements intelligently, you can restore clarity and optimal health.

IMPORTANT TIPS FOR TAKING SUPPLEMENTS

The proper amount of pure vitamins, minerals, amino acids, enzymes, oils, botanicals, and other healing substances complexed as they naturally occur in their living sources contribute to vibrant health and inhibit or reverse many degenerative processes. Many also assist in removal of toxins from the body, including metabolites of conventional drugs. Medications or drugs are toxins too. An article published in the *Journal of the American Medical Association* in June 2000 demonstrated that

---

Note: *The standard dosages on the product label are appropriate unless otherwise stated.* You do not have to take all the supplements listed for each condition at the same time. ***Start with the first three or four products, based on your needs.*** Take supplements as recommended on the bottle or less, for a minimum of one or two months (in severe cases, longer) until relieved of the symptoms. Then lower the supplement dosage for maintenance. Supplements are important for maintaining adequate neuronutrients. Without continued supplemental support, if you have a deficiency, clinical symptoms may reappear. If you would like to obtain further information about these and other supplements, call TOLL FREE 888-340-5888 and request a copy of the complimentary SUPPLEMENT GUIDE or search www.natureshospital.com.

the *fourth leading cause of death* in U.S. hospitals is iatrogenic disease—that is, disease caused by medical treatment.

1. In general, it's best to take your supplements just prior to or with meals because vitamins, minerals, oils, enzymes, and plant medicines are better absorbed with food. Also, there is less chance of heartburn, upset stomach, nausea, diarrhea, or other adverse reactions. However, *the sublingual supplements* (all with "Relief" in their names); need to be dissolved either under the tongue or in the mouth, as indicated on the label.

2. In the beginning take ¼ or ½ of the suggested dosage on the supplement label. This way you can slowly introduce them into your system according to your body's need and tolerance.

3. If you are taking prescription drugs, *don't take* them at the same time you take your nutritional supplements.

4. *Do not* take Brain Igniter or supplements containing B-vitamins at nighttime because they may keep you awake.

5. Any decision to stop using any of your prescription drugs should be made in conjunction with professional guidance.

6. Get appropriate blood tests and check your blood pressure. Keep your blood glucose levels as close to normal as possible.

7. Keep notes on what specific supplements improve your symptoms and general health.

References

Chapter One

Falsetti, S.A., and Davis, J. "The Nonpharmacologic Treatment of Generalized Anxiety Disorder." *Psychiatric Clinics of North America* (2001): 24:99–117.

Hulley, S., et al. "Randomized trial of estrogen plus progestin for secondary prevention of coronary heart disease in postmenopausal women." *JAMA* (1998): 280:605–13.

Kravitz, H.M., Sabelli, H.C., and Fawcett, J. "Dietary supplements of phenylalanine and other amino acid precursors of brain neuroamines in the treatment of depressive disorders." *J Am Osteopath Assoc* (1984): 84:1 Suppl: 119:23.

Mercuro, G., et al. "Effects of acute administration of natural progesterone on peripheral vascular responsiveness in healthy postmenopausal women." *Am J Cardiol* (1999): 84: 2:214–8.

Pauling, L. "Orthomolecular psychiatry: varying the concentrations of substances normally present in the human body may control mental disease." *J Nutr Environmed* (1995); 5:2:187–98.

Russouw, J.E., Anderson, G.L., Prentice, R.L., et al. "Risks and benefits of estrogen plus progestin in healthy postmenopausal women: principal results From the Women's Health Initiative randomized controlled trial." *JAMA* (17 Jul. 2002): 288:3:321–33.

Stampfer, M.J., et al. "Postmenopausal estrogen therapy and cardiovascular disease: ten-year follow up from the Nurses' Health Study." *NEJM* (1991): 325:756–62.

Chapter Two

"Apostle to the Ephesians." *In Ellicott's Commentary on the Whole Bible*. Reprint (8 vols. in 4). Grand Rapids: Zondervan Publishing House, 1981.

Berke, J.D., et al. "Addiction, Dopamine, and the Molecular Mechanisms of Memory." *Neuron* (Mar. 2000): 25:3:515-32.

Bruce, F.F. "The Epistle to the Romans: An Introduction and Commentary." *The Tyndale New Testament Commentaries*. Grand Rapids: Eerdmans, 1963.

Hendriksen, William. "Exposition of Paul's Epistle to the Romans." New Testament Commentary. 2 vols. Grand Rapids: Baker Book House, 1980, 1981.

Simpson, E.K., and Bruce, F.F. "Commentary on the Epistles to the Ephesians and the Colossians." *The New International Commentary on the New Testament*. Grand Rapids: Wm. B. Eerdmans Publishing Co., 1957.

Chapter Three

Beidel, D.C., et al. *Shy Children, Phobic Adults: Nature and Treatment of Social Phobia*. American Psychological Association, 1998.

Brown, S.L., et al. "Providing Social Support May Be More Beneficial than Receiving It: Results from a Prospective Study of Mortality." *Psychological Science* (Jul. 2003): 14:4:320-27.

Rettew, D.C., "Avoidant Personality Disorder, Generalized Social Phobia, and Shyness: Putting the Personality Back into Personality Disorders." *Harvard Review of Psychiatry* (Dec. 2000): 8:6:283–97.

Schneier, F.R., ed, "Social Anxiety Disorder." *Psychiatric Clinics of North America* (Dec. 2001): 24:4.

Stott, John R.W. *Guard the Gospel: The Message of 2 Timothy.* Downers Grove, Ill.: InterVarsity Press, 1973.

Chapter Six

Falsetti, S.A. and Davis, J. "The Nonpharmacologic Treatment of Generalized Anxiety Disorder." *Psychiatric Clinics of North America* (Mar. 2001): 24:1:99–117.

Garnefski, N., et al. "Cognitive Emotion Regulation Strategies and Depressive Symptoms: Differences between Males and Females." *Personality and Individual Differences* (Jan. 2002): 36:2:267–76.

Jetty, P.V., et al. "Neurobiology of Generalized Anxiety Disorder." *Psychiatric Clinics of North America* (Mar. 2001): 24:75–97.

Kendler, K.S., et al. "Toward a Comprehensive Developmental Model for Major Depression in Women." *American Journal of Psychiatry* (Jul. 2002): 159:7:113–45.

Chapter Seven

Bemporad, J.R. "Aspects of Psychotherapy with Adults with Attention Deficit Disorder." *Annals of the New York Academy of Sciences* (Jun. 2001): 931:302–09.

Clarke, A.R., Barry, R.J., McCarthy, R., and Selikowitz, M. "EEG Analysis in Attention-Deficit/Hyperactivity Disorder: A comparative study of two subtypes." *Psychiatry Research* (1998): 81:19–29.

Drake, R.E., et al. "Implementing Dual Diagnosis Services for Clients with Severe Mental Illness." *Psychiatric Services* (Apr. 2001): 52:4:469–76.

John, E.R. "The role of QEEG topographic mapping or 'neurometrics' in the diagnosis of psychiatric and neurological disorders." *Electroencephalography and Clinical Neurophysiology* (1989): 73:2–4.

Jonkman, L.M., Kemner, C., Verbaten, M.N., Koelega, H.S., Camfferman, G., van der Gaag, R.J. et al. "Effects of methylphenidate on event-related potentials and performance of attention-deficit hyperactivity disorder children in auditory and visual selective attention tasks." *Biological Psychiatry* (1997a): 41:690–702.

Khan A., et al. "Symptom Reduction and Suicide Risk in Patients Treated with Placebo in Antidepressant Clinical Trials: An Analysis of the Food and Drug Administration Database." *Archives of General Psychiatry* (Apr. 2000): 57:4:311–17.

Leuchter, A.F., et al. "Changes in Brain Function of Depressed Subjects During Treatment with Placebo." *American Journal of Psychiatry* (Jan. 2002): 159:1:122–29.

Lubar, J.F., and Lubar, J.O. "Neuro-feedback assessment and treatment for attention deficit/hyperactivity disorders." In J.R. Evans & A. Abarbanel (Eds.), *Introduction to quantitative EEG and neuro-feedback* (1999): 103–143. San Diego: Academic Press.

Moncrieff, J. "The Antidepressant Debate." *British Journal of Psychiatry* (Mar. 2002): 180:3:193–94.

Richardson, R.D. and Engel, C.C. Jr. "Evaluation and management of medically unexplained physical symptoms." *Neurologist* (Jan. 2004): 10:18–30.

Thompson, M. and Thompson, L. *The Neuro-feedback Book,* Association for Applied Psychophysiology and Biofeedback, 2003.

Wilens, T.E., et al. "Attention Deficit/Hyperactivity Disorder Across the Lifespan," *Annual Review of Medicine* (2002): 53:113–31.

Chapter Eight

Ben-Menachem, E. "Vagus Nerve Stimulation, Side Effects, and Long-Term Safety." *Journal of Clinical Neurophysiology* (Sept. 2001): 18:5:415–18.

Evans, W.E., et al. "Pharmacogenomics-Drug Disposition, Drug Targets, and Side Effects." *New England Journal of Medicine* (6 Feb. 2003): 348:6:538–49.

Glassman, A.H. and Sharpio, P.A. "Depression and the Course of Coronary Artery Disease." *American Journal of Psychiatry* (Jan. 1998): 155:1:4–11.

Guttmacher, A.E., et al. "Genomic Medicine—A Primer," *New England Journal of Medicine* (7 Nov. 2002): 347:19:1512–20.

Kirsch, D.L., and Smith, R.B. "Cranial electrotherapy stimulation for anxiety, depression, insomnia, cognitive dysfunction, and pain." In Paul Rosch (Ed.), *Bioelectromagnetic Medicine:* 727–740. New York: Marcel Dekker, 2004.

Marangell, L.B., et al. "Vagus Nerve Stimulation (VNS) for Major Depressive Episodes: One-Year Outcomes," *Biological Psychiatry* (15 Feb. 2002): 51:4:280–87.

McGuffin, P., et al, Eds. *Psychiatric Genetics and Genomics.* Oxford University Press, 2002.

Merikangas, K.R., et al. "Will the Genomics Revolution Revolutionize Psychiatry?" *American Journal of Psychiatry* (Apr. 2003): 160:4:625–35.

Murphy, G.M., Jr., et al. "Pharmacogenetics of Antidepressant Medication Intolerance." *American Journal of Psychiatry* (Oct. 2003): 160:10:1830–35.

Pollak, S.D., et al. "Early Experience Is Associated with the Development of Categorical Representations for Facial Expressions of Emotion." *Proceedings of the National Academy of Sciences* (25 Jun. 2002): 99:13:9072–76.

Rugulies, R. "Depression as a Predictor for Coronary Heart Disease: A review and Meta-Analysis." *American Journal of Preventive Medicine* (Jul. 2002): 23:1:51–61.

Sackeim, H.A., et al. "Vagus Nerve Stimulation (VNS) for Treatment-Resistant Depression: Efficacy, Side Effects, and Predictors of Outcome." *Neuropsychopharmacology* (Nov.

Smith, T.W. and Ruiz, J.M. "Psychosocial influences on the Development and Course of Coronary Heart Disease: Current Status and Implications for Research and Practice." *Journal of Consulting and Clinical Psychology* (Jun. 2002): 70:3:548–68.

Vastag, B. "Gene Chips Inch toward the Clinic." *JAMA* (8 Jan. 2003): 289:2:155–59.

Chapter Nine

Bonnesen, C., Eggleston, I.M., and Hayes, J.D. "Dietary indoles and isothiocyanates that are generated from cruciferous vegetables can both stimulate apoptosis and confer protection against DNA damage in human colon cell lines." *Cancer Res.* (15 Aug. 2001): 61:16:6120–30.

Chang, E.T., Smedby, K.E., Zhang, S.M., et al. "Dietary factors and risk of non-Hodgkin lymphoma in men and women." *Cancer Epidemiol Biomarkers Prev.* (Feb. 2005): 14:2:512–20.

Chen, L., Stacewicz-Sapuntzakis, M., Duncan, C., et al. "Oxidative DNA damage in prostate cancer patients consuming tomato sauce-based entrees as a whole-food intervention." *J Natl Cancer Inst* (2001): 93:1872–9.

Correa Lima, M.P. and Gomes-da-Silva, M.H. "Colorectal cancer: lifestyle and dietary factors." *Nutr Hosp.* (Jul. 2005): 20:4: 235–41.

Dietary Phytochemicals in Cancer Prevention and Treatment, Advances in Experimental Medicine and Biology (1996): 401: 87–100.

Docherty, J.P., Sack, D.A., Roffman, M., Finch, M., and Komorowski, J.R. "A double-blind, placebo-controlled, exploratory trial of chromium picolinate in atypical depression: effect on carbohydrate craving." *J Psychiatr Pract* (2005): 11:5:302–14.

Gorham, E.D., Garland, C.F., Garland, F.C., et al. "Vitamin D and prevention of colorectal cancer." *J Steroid Biochem Mol Biol.* (15 Oct. 2005). 2001): 25: 5:713–28.

Kucuk, O., Sarkar, F.H., Djuric, Z., et al. "Effects of lycopene supplementation in patients with localized prostate cancer." *Exp Biol Med* (2002): 227:881–5.

Larsson, S.C., Rafter J., Holmberg L., Bergkvist L., and Wolk A. "Red meat consumption and risk of cancers of the proximal colon, distal colon and rectum: the Swedish Mammography Cohort." *Int J Cancer.* (20 Feb. 2005): 113:5:829–34.

McDougall, J., Litzau, K., Haver, E., Saunders, V., and Spiller, G.A. "Rapid reduction of serum cholesterol and blood pressure by a twelve-day, very low-fat, strictly vegetarian diet." *J Am Coll Nutr.* (5 Oct. 1995): 14:5:491–6.

Nothlings, U., Wilkens, L.R., Murphy, S.P., et al. "Meat and fat intake as risk factors for pancreatic cancer: the multiethnic cohort study." J *Natl Cancer Inst.* (5 Oct. 2005): 97:19:1458–65.

O'Dwyer, S.T., Smith, R.J., Hwang, T.L., and Wilmore, D.W. "Maintenance of small bowel mucosa with glutamine-enriched parenteral nutrition." *JPEN J Parenter Enteral Nutr.* (13 Nov. 1989): 13:6:579–85.

Ornish, D., Weidner, G., Fair, W.R., et al. "Intensive lifestyle changes may affect the progression of prostate cancer." *J Urol.;* discussion 1069–70. (17 Sep. 2005): 174:33:1065–9.

Park, Y.J., Volpe, S.L., and Decker, F.A. "Quantitation of carnosine in humans' plasma after dietary consumption of beef." *J Agric Food Chem.* (15 Jun. 2005): 53:12:4736–9.

Rose, P., Faulkner, K., Williamson, G., and Mithen, R. "7-Methylsulfinylheptyl and 8-methylsulfinyloctyl isothiocyanates from watercress are potent inducers of phase II enzymes." *Carcinogenesis.* (2 Nov. 2000): 21:11:1983–8.

Schulze, M.B., Hoffmann, K., Manson, J.E., et al. "Dietary pattern, inflammation, and incidence of type 2 diabetes in women." *Am J Clin Nutr.* (Sep 2005): 82:3:675–84.

Walker, M., Aronson, K.J., King, W., et al. "Dietary patterns and risk of prostate cancer in Ontario, Canada." *Int J Cancer* (10 Sep. 2005): 116:4:592–8.

Chapter Ten

Amsden, David. *Pop. Snort. Parachute.* (4 Oct. 2004): 24–31.

Baethge, C. "Long-Term Treatment of Schizoaffective Disorder: Review and Recommendations." *Pharmacopsychiatry* (Mar./Apr. 2003): 36:2:45–56.

Ballenger, J.C., et al. (International Consensus Group on Depression and Anxiety) "Consensus Statement on Generalized Anxiety Disorder from the International Consensus Group on Depression and Anxiety." *Journal of Clinical Psychiatry* (2003): 62: Supp. 11:53–58.

Braham, R., Dawson, B., and Goodman, C. "The effect of glucosamine supplementation on people experiencing regular knee pain." *Br J Sports Med* (Feb 2003): 37:1:45–9.

Cangiano, C., Laviano, A., Del Ben, M., Preziosa, I., Angelico, F., Cascino, A., and Rossi-Fanelli, F. "Effects of oral

5-hydroxy-tryptophan on energy intake and macronutrient selection in non-insulin dependant diabetic patients." *Int J Obes Relat Metab Disord* (Jul. 1998): 22:7:648–54.

Carroll, D.N., and Roth, M.T. "Evidence for the cardioprotective effects of omega-3 fatty acids." *Annals of Pharmacotherapy* (2002): 36:1950–1956.

Christen, S., Woodall, A.A., Shigenaga, M.K., Southwell-Kelly, P.T., Duncan, M.W., and Ames, B.N. "Gamma-tocopherol traps mutagenic electrophiles such as NO(X) and complements alpha-tocopherol: physiological implications." *Proc Natl Acad Sci USA.* (Apr. 1997): 94:7:3217–22.

Edwards, K.R., Hershey, L., Bednarczyk, E.M., Lichter, D., Farlow, M., and Johnson, S. "Efficacy and safety of Galantamine in patients with dementia with Lewy bodies: a 12-week interim analysis." *Dement Geriatr Cogn Discnd* (2004): 17: Supp I: 40–8.

Faraone, S.V., et al. "Attention-Deficit/Hyperactivity Disorder in Adults: An Overview," *Biological Psychiatry* (1 Jul.. 2000): 48:1:9–20.

Fombonne, E. "The Prevalence of Autism." *Journal of the American Medical Association* (1 Jan. 2003): 289:1:87–89.

Garg, A.K., Berg, R.A., Silver, F.H., and Garg, H.G. "Effect of proteoglycans on type 1 collagen fibre formation." *Biomaterials* (Aug. 1989): 10:6:413–419.

Glassman, A.H. and Shapiro, P.A. "Depression and the Course of Coronary Artery Disease." *American Journal of Psychiatry* (Jan. 1998): 155:1:4–11.

Hallowell, E.M. and Ratey, J.J. *Driven to Distraction.* New York: Pantheon Books, 1994.

Hipkiss, A.R., Brownson, C., and Carrier, M.J. "Carnosine, the anti-ageing, anti-oxidant dipeptide, may react with protein carbonyl groups." *Mech Ageing Dev* (15 Sep. 2001): 122:13:1431–45.

Hoffer, Abram. *Orthomolecular Medicine for Physicians.* New Canaan, Conn: Keats Publishing, 1989.

Koob, G.F., et al. "Neurobiological Mechanisms in the Transition from Drug Use to Drug Dependence." *Neuroscience and Biobehavioral Reviews* (Jan. 2004): 27:8:739–49.

Lazarou, J., Pomeranz, B.H., and Corey, P.N. "Incidence of adverse drug reactions in hospitalized patients: a meta-analysis of prospective studies." *JAMA* (1998): 279:15:1200–5.

Marinacci, Barbara, Ed. *Pauling, Linus in His own Words: Selections from Writings, Speeches, and Interviews.* New York: Simon and Schuster, 1995.

Mohr, D.C., et al. "Association between stressful life events and exacerbation in multiple sclerosis: A meta-analysis." *Bio Medical Journal* (27 Mar. 2004): 328:731.

Murav'ev lu, V., Venikova, M.S., Pleskovskaia, G.N., Riazantseva, T.A., and Sigidin, laA. "Effect of dimethyl sulfoxide and dimethyl sulfone on a destructive process in the joints of mice with spontaneous arthritis." *Patol Fiziol Eksp Ter* (Mar. 1991): 2:37–39.

Murphy, Gm, Jr., et al. "Pharmacogenetics of Antidepressant Medication Intolerance." *American Journal of Psychiatry* (Oct. 2003): 160:10:1830–35.

Nestler, E.J. "Total Recall—the Memory of Addiction." *Science* (22 Jun. 2001): 292:5525:2266–67.

O'Connell, D.F. and Beyer. E., Eds. *Managing the Dually Diagnosed Patient: Current Issues and Clinical Approaches*, Second Edition. Bridgehampton, New York: Haworth Press, 2002.

Perry, P., et al. "Testosterone Therapy in Late-Life Major Depression in Males." *Journal of Clinical Psychiatry* (Dec. 2002): 63:12:1096–1101.

Pfeiffer, Carl. *Nutrition and Mental Illness.* Rochester, Vt.: Healing Arts Press, 1975.

Pichichero, M.E., et al. "Mercury Concentrations and Metabolism in Infants Receiving Vaccines Containing

Thiomersal: A Descriptive Study." *Lancet* (20 Nov. 2002): 360:9347:1737–41.

Pollak, S.D., et al. "Early Experience Is Associated with the Development of Categorical Representations for Facial Expressions of Emotion," Proceedings of the National Academy of Sciences. (25 Jun. 2002): 99:13:9072–76.

"Practice Guideline for the Treatment of Patients with Schizophrenia." *AM J Psychiatry* (Feb. 2004): 161:2, Suppl.

Ridker, P.M., Rifai, N., Rose, L., Buring, J.E., and Cook, N.R. "Comparison of C-reactive protein and low-density lipoprotein cholesterol levels in the prediction of first cardiovascular events." *New England Journal of Medicine* (2003): 347:1557–1565.

Rugulies, R. "Depression as a Predictor for Coronary Heart Disease: A Review and Meta-Analysis," *American Journal of Preventive Medicine* (Jul. 2002): 23:1:51–61.

Serbinova, E., Kagan, V., Han, D., and Packer, L. "Free radical recycling and intramembrane mobility in the antioxidant properties of alpha-tocopherol and alpha-tocotrienol." *Free Radic Biol Med.* (1991): 10:5:293–75.

Stoll, A.L., et al. "Omega 3 Fatty Acids in Bipolar Disorder: A Preliminary Double-Blind, Placebo-Controlled Trial." *Archives of General Psychiatry* (May 1999): 56:5:407–12.

Tiemeier, H., van Tuijl, H.R., Hofman, A., Kiliaan, A.J., and Breteler, M.M. "Plasma fatty acid composition and depression are associated in the elderly: the Rotterdam study." *Am J Clin Nutr.* (Jul. 2003): 78:1:40–6.

Vastag, B. "Gene Chips Inch toward the Clinic," *JAMA* (8 Jan. 2003): 289:2:155–59.

Vitiello, B. and Lederhendler, I. "Research on Eating Disorders: Current Status and Future Prospects," *Biological Psychiatry* (2000): 47:9:777–86.

Wasserstein, J., et al., Eds. "Adult Attention Deficit Disorder: Brain Mechanisms and Life Outcomes," *Annals of the New York Academy of Sciences* (Jun. 2001): 931.

Waters, E., et al. "Role of taurine in preventing acetamino-phen-induced hepatic injury in the rat." *Am J Physiol Gastrointest Liver Physiol* (Jun. 2001): 280:6:G1274–9

Yeargin-Allsop, M., et al. "Prevalence of Autism in a U.S. Metropolitan Area." *Journal of the American Medical Association* (1 Jan. 2003): 289:1:49–55.

Zlotnick, C., et al. "Postpartum Depression in Women Receiving Public Assistance: Pilot Study of an Interpersonal-Therapy-Oriented Group Intervention." *American Journal of Psychiatry* (Apr. 2001): 158:4:638–40.

Appendices

LABORATORIES

For those who suffer chronic and severe neurotransmitter imbalances, following is a list of laboratories for more specialized testing of neurotransmitters.

If you suspect imbalance in your hormones, find an endocrinologist who is skilled and knowledgeable to measure and give you the correct level of hormones. You also need to be monitored from time to time through urine, saliva or a blood test, if you have any special needs.

Company	*Tests Performed*
DBS Labs, Inc.	Urine
8723 Falcon St.	Neurotransmitter Tests
Duluth, MN 55808	
877.476.7229	
www.labdbs.com	

Metametrix   Amino Acid Assays
4855 Peachtree Industrial Blvd.   Serum histamine
Suite 201   Pyrroles
Norcross, GA 30092
800.221.4640
www.metametrix.com

Doctors Data Inc.   Hair analysis
3755 Illinois Avenue
St. Charles, IL 60174
800.323.2784

Index

C

D

R

About the Author

C. Samuel Verghese, MD (AM) PhD, DAAPM, BCIA (EEG), DAPA, has more than 40 years of experience in holistic medicine. His investigation of the interrelationship of brain biochemistry, mind, spirituality, and physical health began in adolescence. His journey has taken him to many educational institutions (including Harvard University) and spiritual communities which over the years equipped him to serve people with challenging needs. Beginning in the 1970s he had the privilege of conducting workshops across the United States on many topics, among them brain chemistry, stress management, and natural Christian approaches to health care and spiritual development. His quest to discover new botanical healing remedies recently took him to the rain forest of South America. Throughout his journey—as researcher and perennial student of life, devoted husband and father of three, author, clinician, formulator of nutritional supplements, college professor, Christian medical missionary, and minister, Dr. Verghese has doggedly pursued his passion to heal and lead his fellow travelers to God.

—James F. Claire, D.O.

Author contact info

Dr. C. Samuel Verghese

Web site:
www. info@biofeedbacknj.com

Toll Free: 1.888.661.2827

How Can You Help?

If the Holy Spirit is stirring you to join us in establishing a comprehensive Christ-Centered wellness facility for balancing the brain and body and assisting those who struggle with the burden of disease and mental dysfunction, pray for this ministry. We need volunteer doctors, nurses, and numerous other kinds of spiritual and practical help.

Please write to:

Nature's Hospital
P.O. Box 217
Glendora, NJ 08029
1.888.340.5888
1.888.661.2827
www.natureshospital.com